130 COUNTRIES.

When I first got the idea to include contributors from my network in this book, I never imagined that 130 countries would respond to the call. This is indeed solid and pure evidence of the true and massive power of networking.

To the contributors, who are also my friends, by sharing your networking thoughts, advice, success stories, you have inspired me beyond comprehension and have helped make this publication a global masterpiece, something I could have never done without you. You not only took time out of your life to assist me, you also used your voice to encourage and ignite others around the world. I remain in awe of the human connection we all share no matter how far apart we are. I am now even more determined to continue connecting the world through networking for the greater good.

We are living proof of every word in this book.
Living proof that all things are possible, and that together through networking, we are unlimited.

Thank you for being a part of this moment, this mission, this movement, and history.

-Germaine Moody

THE 40 LAWS OF NETWORKING

Keys to creating global Influence, Wealth and Power.

Germaine Moody

become endless

INTERNATIONAL

ISBN 978-0-578-92127-3

Books may be purchased for education, business, or sales promotional use. For book/author inquiries, including bulk orders, contact BecomeEndlessPublishing@gmail.com.

CONTENTS

MY DISCOVERY

People are your greatest resource. The more people resources you have, the fewer limits you will experience in your lifetime.

As we prepare to take off from Atlanta's Hartsfield-Jackson airport headed to Los Angeles, I now realize that I've discovered one of the simplest yet most powerful secrets in the world. I've spent the last twelve months in lounges, cafes, clubs and restaurants meeting thousands of people from every culture and ethnicity, in some of the world's largest cities, across multiple countries. The opportunities, access, endorsements, partnerships, knowledge, ideas and friendships that I've gained from this is beyond phenomenal. What is that secret? It's networking, and apart from God, I owe it all to networking. Networking has not only changed my life, it has given me more life. To me networking means meeting great people, learning about their life and pursuits, providing assistance to them wherever and whenever possible, and them returning the favor, creating a win-win for all. The connections you make will be for the current moment, future moments or for a lifetime. You'll never know how incredibly beneficial they can be to your life until you start meeting them. People are your greatest resource. The more people resources you have, the fewer limitations you will experience in your lifetime.

There's nothing wrong with wanting more, because with more, you can be more and you can do more for yourself and others. We can have more of everything on this planet except one thing though, and that one thing is time. We are limited, very limited, with time, therefore networking must be used to save time, while allowing you to speed up everything else. Networking allows you to manipulate time to your advantage. The world is moving fast and people are networking every day. That next job or big opportunity you want could appear in an instant by networking or disappear by a lack thereof. There are billions of people swimming in the networking pool. Social media has destroyed degrees of separation. Networking has crippled the rules and annihilated time doctrines, disrupting what was once heavily guarded by opening doors to close knit circles through one new connection.

Without access, dreams will not be fulfilled, goals will not be accomplished. Before we can discuss networking on any level, the benefits and its power, we must first understand and appreciate this new era now upon us, one with doors wide open, where the world is in the palm of your hands. Access has been granted. This access arrived via a surge of in-person events and social meetups around the world, and with a massive new wave of technology that leaves no room for excuses or a lack of knowledge. In past decades we'd have to travel here and there to be with someone in a meeting or to sign and seal a business deal, that day is no longer. Though nothing will ever replace the necessity of face-to-face human interaction, it has become optional in many cases where it it's not mandatory. From networking events to the immeasurable impact of the internet, from smartphones to instant global advertising & marketing, our access to reach each other near and far has been made as easy as the click of a button. We are living in a privileged generation, a clear atmosphere of possibilities, yet only those who take advantage of it will enjoy the fruits. Those who take heed to this extraordinary access and then use it to become a master networker, they will be a part of the chosen few who will be granted a life of unlimited possibilities.

Success is a clever, time-sensitive game, so is networking. If you don't know the rules, you'll never be wise enough to play. If you aren't wise enough to play, you'll never win. In "The 40 Laws of Networking", I'll teach you how to dominate at networking and how to use networking to become influential, wealthy and powerful, while creating a legacy to be proud of. I've invited some of my friends from around the world in 130 countries to join me and to cheer you on.

THE 40 LAWS OF NETWORKING

GERMAINE MOODY

Words.

The power of words is something you must give supreme attention to. They can birth you, advance you, even kill you. Words are used by the poorest and the richest, by the ignorant and the wisest. With all, they still carry the same force. Become a student of words, dedicating the rest of your life to learning their ability, purpose and timing. If not, your life will be limited, without balance and guidance, suffering from a lack of knowledge, deprived of advancement and opportunity. If you do not become a student of words, the majority of your networking will fall on deaf ears.

LAW 1
MASTER WORDS

A master of words is a master of people.

Apart from the sun providing light and power, the water providing nourishment and cleansing, and animals and plants being providing a source of food, we run the entire world, seven days a week, by words. Work, transportation, restaurants, paying bills, interviews, church, school, directions, vacation, business meetings, phone calls, texts, dinner dates, neighbors, shopping, I think you get my point. We use words every single day and just about every hour while awake. It's practically impossible to live without words. Networking is word-driven. What you say and how you say it at the start is what normally gets the contact or person to respond or continue with you. Consider thinking longer before you speak, type, write or text. Develop words and sentences that would generate and persuade the response that you want. Words have personality, which means your communication has a countenance that can be seen and felt without a physical face in view. I suggest you keep a storage of optimistic words on hand and in mind when networking and expanding. People are most attracted to positivity, so maintain that in all of your dealings.

Before you reach out via any communication to network, secure an opportunity or obtain a new contact, make sure you observe and analyze the person, situation and opportunity first. From there you can strategize your words from the information gathered, and begin to create your bait for the catch. Keeping in mind that positivity and optimism, even excitement at times (but don't overdo it), is what most successful people are drawn to. Also understand that the majority of the world operates by perception, that is, by how they feel from what they observe, know, hear, see, etc and by how you make them feel from the words you use. The key is to master the art of cultivating their perception of you, then they will gladly open every door that you can imagine. A master of words is a master of people.

Thoughts from Algeria

"Networking is a valuable way to gain knowledge, learn from the success and mistakes of others, meet potential partners and prospects, raise your profile, learn more about yourself, your business and beyond and get out of the bubble we often enclose ourselves in under the false impression of being busy and remaining focused."
-*Karim Djerboa, Managing Director*

Success from Panama

"Networking has brought me a great team, JV partners, our initial clients and great investors. I would have no business without taking part in events that led to networking."
-*Sydney Tremayne, Founder, Chairman & Investment Strategist*

Advice from Netherlands

"Be open and genuinely interested. Always present yourself as someone who wants to help and contribute something and not as someone who is just looking for opportunities for their own interest."

-Dave Klop, COO at 24EDM

GERMAINE MOODY

LAW 2
WORDS ARE MORE POWERFUL
THAN MONEY

*Words are the most powerful thing on Earth, even more powerful
than the money some think runs the world.*

Never let excess amounts of money or currency fool you of its power. It is only as mighty as our words that accompany its usage or purpose. Money cannot work or operate by itself, it must be directed, and clear direction only comes in the form of words. Most of the money we have now would have never entered our lives without some form of words being used in order to lead it our way. Whether it started from a job interview, negotiating it, or just asking for it, words played a role in receiving it. This proves that words carry more weight, access, opportunity and promise than we tend to give them credit for.

I've fallen in love with words, you must also as soon as possible. Words are shocking, convincing, generous, angering, informative, revealing, saddening, terrifying, persuasive. They can produce every emotion known to man, and instantly instigate any type of resource. What on Earth is more powerful? Other than God, absolutely nothing. Even He used words to create everything, so words have to be next in the power line. Knowing this, words should be the first focal point for networking. They must become a mandatory concern, otherwise your networking will lack in connection value, your multicultural and continental reach will be limited, and your time will be wasted. Wasted words is a waste of time. Wasted time is wasted money. People often say that "Action speaks louder than words". Action may speak louder but without words, the majority of all action wouldn't know how or where to begin. Words are the most powerful thing on Earth, even more powerful than the money some think runs the world.

Thoughts from Trinidad

"Networking is about making connections; building and enduring mutually beneficial relationships. It is the single most powerful marketing tactic to accelerate and sustain success for any individual or organisation."
-Shayanne Friday, Student

Advice from Jamaica

"The best networking comes from genuine relationships, not a business card exchange. No matter whom you're trying to build a relationship with, treating that person as a friend rather than a business contact will take you much further with the relationship."
-Anthony Wood, CEO, Bustamante Hospital For Children

LAW 3

SPEAK WITH CLARITY

Know who you're dealing with so you'll know how to deal.

The next important asset when it comes to networking will be your ability to communicate properly. The greater your communication skills are and your awareness of the communication skill level of those you will interact with, the better off you will be. This is why it is important to observe and study other people, races and cultures. I often say "Know who you're dealing with so you'll know how to deal." This can prove to be very rewarding for you. People judge from the outside first, what they see and hear. As far as what they hear, it is vital that you are able to clearly articulate and translate verbally what it is you desire to accomplish. In many networking scenarios, your initial conversation will focus on similarities and the things both parties or individuals are passionate about. People feed on great responses when networking, they gravitate towards those who not only listen carefully to what they're saying but also responds in a way that adds to where they left off. This is part of the seduction in the game of networking. To be able to express yourself with clarity in your words, using words to your advantage to attract, intrigue and seduce, you will become a master of words, which makes you a master of those who receive your words. Of course we're not out to brainwash or mentally enslave others when networking but there is a seductive power in networking that cannot be denied, especially when meeting in person.

Networking is all communication, whether it's by writing or speaking, you need to know how to do both well for ultimate success. Some people network better in person because they have enhanced social skills that allow them to be relaxed and very approachable, even drawing crowds by their mere presence. Others fare better with writing. Either way, words are crucial. If meeting a new potential business partner for lunch in person, your choice of words can either further the business relationship or end it before you finish eating. I often practice conversations with myself before business phone calls and before meeting others in person. It could be weeks, days or even just 10 minutes before, but it works and it helps. Try this yourself to help ease anxiety, to get a boost of confidence or to feel more prepared. There are also days when I just wing it but that only happens when I have multiple calls back to back, wherein the topic is about the same thing, just with different people.

Enhancing your vocabulary, reading, watching great interviews, each of these prepare you to speak with clarity and master words for networking. Some people won't even respond to you if your communication and choice of words aren't up to par. It's happened to me in the past and I've done it before when approached unprofessionally by another person. Observation is the key though. The next time you're scheduled to meet someone in person or have a call, make it a point to follow their lead, listen and observe. If you're in charge of leading the call then always keep an open door for questions and for the other person or group to chime in. Pay close attention to the vocabulary and how the person flows. Respond appropriately, making them feel comfortable so there's an ongoing give and take that uplifts, encourages and expands the conversation while still focusing on the subject and purpose. When you do this, you will get some of the best opportunities and have some of the best conversations, best friendships and best business relationships ever. That is what you should desire from networking, the best of everything, because it's readily available through the right people resources. Only the best should be allowed to come in and remain in your immediate circle, the rest can be put aside for later or completely dismissed.

Thoughts from Romania

"We're born to be social beings, to interact with other people, so networking is a part of everyday life. It helps us make the most of our core assets and puts us in connection with other people that can complement what we've got."

-Flavius Saracut, CMO Mobiversal

Success from Japan

"It has been only through participating actively in the community in which I operate that I have been able to make connections that now drive my business. My clients come to me through friends I have made over the years mingling with various Chambers of Commerce, not-for profit groups and business associations. Depending on how broadly you define networking, I believe that virtually all of my networks began initially through some form of social interaction in the business community."

-Patricia Bader-Johnston, CEO

GERMAINE MOODY

LAW 4
WRITE WITH STRATEGY

The written word has immeasurable power. Words are everywhere. Around the house, on your way to work, school, notice the words on appliances, mail, signs, your cell phone, advertisements, cars, buildings, even clothing. We can't get away from words, they occupy more places than actual people. This is another reason I can conclude that words are the most powerful thing on Earth. And this is also why they must become a staple in your networking pursuits. When preparing any type of messages, email, business document, and so on, each and every word you use can and will determine the outcome you desire or the response that will follow. No more writing as usual, those days must end today. Now you should start thinking strategically before you write your next message. Take time to calculate words that not only get your point across but also those that activate an emotional response. We are emotional by nature. If you can tap into and then direct the emotions of a person, you will conquer them.

Advertisements on television, in magazines, newspapers, out in public, and on the internet have mastered the art of emotional selling using words. This should also be applied in your networking. In addition to sticking to the point, if you can enhance what you write by adding a sense of excitement, desire and value, or assurance of your interest in the matter, your chances of getting positive responses and being successful will be greater. Take greeting cards for example, a $7.5 billion dollar industry that is operated and ingeniously seduced by words. There may be a few drawings on some of the cards but the words themselves carry the weight, delivers the goods, and makes the sale. People buy greetings cards by the billions to express their thoughts, often in words they weren't able to think of themselves. Cards that sell the most are written by individuals or teams that have mastered words. Learn from them, even if you have to go buy a few cards this week to study, this will enhance your skills. Whatever it takes on your part, whether it's examining the works of other writers and authors or reviewing previous conversations with colleagues to see how you could have responded better, be steadfast at mastering words so you can create more than just contacts and business connections but also produce loyal followers and colleagues who are ready and willing to help you accomplish anything imaginable.

Thoughts from Bhutan

"Networking is important because the entire ecosystem of the world is so widely exposed that everyone is dependent on others in one way or another. Networking is also important because people need feedback to grow and improve. Feedback is the breakfast of champions."
-Om Nirola, Associate Director, Druk Holding & Investments

Advice from Dominica

"First you have to think of what you want. Secondly, who is your target market of individuals of groups that you need to connect to. Thirdly, what mediums should you use to network. Fourthly, build your network. And fifthly, execute and don't just sit there and wait, you have to keep at it on a daily basis to make sure you get positive feedback and results."
-Cheryl Emanuel-Plummer, CEO

Influence.

Who are you becoming? What can you introduce or make better? Will they listen to you in the city? Will they follow you around the world? Your influence will be obvious or invisible, there is no middle ground. Influence alone gives you the ability to gain wealth, power, and respect. You need no other ticket for the ride. Don't be surprised when others begin to envy you, it is all-inclusive with the deal. Your influence must be strategically planned and monitored in the contest of networking. It can deceptively create a different image on its own if you don't keep watch.

LAW 5

CREATE YOUR ONLINE PROFILE

We now live on the internet, which means it is imperative that you have an online identity or profile to expand your networking. Today, everyone is on Facebook, Linkedin, Twitter, Instagram, Snapchat or affiliated with a variety of other social networks, apps and websites, making it conclusive that your online identity may be the most important thing you need to establish. In addition to your own personal website, blogs, press releases and so forth, creating online profiles on more professional-oriented social networks will have endless benefits for networking. There are three main identities that you need to include in your online profile that we'll briefly discuss. I recommend that you have at least one online profile account that you update periodically or as needed. Linkedin is my preferred choice as of this writing, and it is the leading professional network.

Business Identity

This identity consists of where you've worked or currently work, the type of skills you have, if you work for yourself, how long you've held job positions and so forth. Though all of these matter tremendously, the most important thing in your Business Identity will be your current titles such as CEO, Chef, Executive Intern, Lead Supervisor, Manager, MBA Candidate, etc. Your titles are your most powerful asset when creating your online identity because people respond to titles. Why is this? It's simple, perception. When networking, we all want to connect to those who appear to be leaders, those who we believe can make things happen. Your business identity alone can create that perception for you, instantly, and enhance your connections and networking power. Make sure all of your titles sound as profound and valuable as possible. If you're the main Cook at a restaurant, though not considered a Chef, update your title to "Executive Cook", "Lead Cook", or "Chief Cook". If you just have "Student" on your profile, change that to "Highly Focused Student" or "Student On A Mission". There are several ways to enhance your title to your advantage so that you appeal to others at first glance because second glances are uncommon.

In addition to spicing up your titles, any recommendations and endorsements relating to your business identity are priceless. Of course recommendations in the other two identities are great, but those pertaining to your business identity carry the greatest clout. Whether they are based on actual past business relationships you had with the person recommending you or not, they are still valuable. Most marketing and advertising of anything or anyone is full of propaganda anyway. Now don't get me wrong, your information needs to be truthful because at some point you may have to account for what's in it. Receiving recommendations from others in your industry or in the industries you desire to get into always helps. Endorsements from the right people can open up the entire world to you overnight, so don't take this lightly. Using the affiliated credibility given from your connections to your advantage is the sign of a networking pro.

Community Identity

For this identity you want to list organizations, associations and any non-profits that you are affiliated with, frequent contributor to, volunteered for or a member of. If you've held any leadership positions with these organizations, list those as well. You should consider requesting written recommendations from someone on their executive team that you can include on your profile also. This identity is very important because it shows that you care about those around you. Power connections want to see that you're doing something humanitarian with your life, influence and success.

Global Identity

For this identity, you want to list affiliations that deal specifically with another country, be it work, community, government, academia, philanthropic, etc. Make sure you include the country's name in the description. Recommendations from friends and colleagues outside of your country are great assets. Make sure they specify their region of the world in their recommendation of you. Also, authors are respected worldwide, so if you're an author, include your book titles in your profile. Books give you automatic leadership credibility as someone who has something to say with some level of expertise. Power connections respect and are attracted to people who use their voice and platform to empower others. Overall, your strategy should be to create an online profile that is attractive, approachable, impressive, enticing and one that will generate the interest, connections and opportunities that you desire.

Create A Powerful Perception

Perception is everything. It is simply an awareness of the senses or the mind; to be made aware of something or someone. The success or failure of your networking will all come down to perception, it is crucial. Luckily, you get to co-orchestrate the perception you desire others to have of you. Though you can't decide their perception, you can indeed influence it, just like billion dollar corporations do to consumers every day. Perception can present, open or close doors. This means, in order to achieve maximum influence, wealth and power through networking, you must use all resources, strategies and tactics to create an appealing and magnetic picture of yourself in the minds of others.

In influential circles around the world, perceptions of integrity, kindness, hard-working, smart, innovative, resourceful, reliable, knowledgeable and successful are looked upon highly. People must perceive as many of or all of these about you as possible. If you are not already widely known or connected, your online identity can be the starting point to achieve this. Your communication, descriptions, connections, videos, photos, products, services, testimonials, awards and recognitions, associations, recommendations and so on creates perception. The more strategic content and communication you share, the more it will penetrate the minds of those that see, hear, read and experience it, and thus influence their perception of you. Whatever type of people you desire to connect with, that is the perception you should aim to create. Increasing intensity, size and repetition will furthermore maximize your perception creating goals. You should also consider observing how you perceive those that you admire and desire to be like. While still being authentic to your values and personality, take notes and then duplicate some of their perception approaches, campaigns, devices, strategies or tactics in order to get similar results.

Thoughts from India

"Time was when one had to physically scour (his part of) the world looking for opportunities and like-minded people to collaborate with. Today, thanks to the Internet, one can work with whomsoever one likes and release his products and wares in a market of his or her choice. All with a click of the mouse. This then is the networking world and it makes sense to work/associate with people who are equally passionate about creating something meaningful and tangible. To me Networking allows my footprints to be global. A single geography, demography, culture, class...these are passe."

-Raj Viswanadha, Children's And Adult (Crime Fiction) Author

Success from Somalia

"I worked for Somaliland National Youth Umbrella (SONYO). The power of networking was applied by colleagues to influence all politicians to change their view and support youth political participation in Somaliland. We also built a new building for SONYO, plus lobbied and succeeded to start Somaliland Youth Development Fund where the incumbent President Silanyo endorsed a decree in 2014. This will allow different levels of government, businesses, international organizations and other NGOs to allocate money for the Somaliland National Youth Fund and mainstream youth agendas in their work and the country as a whole."

-Yahya Mohamed Abdi, Project Assistant

Advice from Georgia

"Build an online presence and reach out to people actively. Cool opportunities are hiding in every corner of the internet, not only in the mainstream websites such as LinkedIn, but also in small forums, blogs, their comment sections. Just register wherever something looks interesting and start talking to everyone!"

-Sandro Kipiani, Entrepreneur/Marketer

GERMAINE MOODY

LAW 6
BUILD ALLIANCES

To limit your influence is to waste your entire life.

The quickest way to increase your influence and to enhance your credibility is by establishing strategic alliances. Connecting with the right people, organizations and businesses in the right regions, industries and sectors, at the right time, is absolutely crucial to your influence. Believe it or not, you are one connection away from everything your heart could ever dream of, but it takes work, research, precision, patience, and action. Alliances can keep you in the game, even when the referee tries to throw you out. Alliances can cover your back and make you appear larger or even smarter than you really are. The more great alliances you obtain, the more influential you will become. Everyone wants to be connected to influential people. Whether you like them, love them, agree with them or not, influential people matter. They can sell just about anything, they can persuade the emotions and decisions of the masses, some can even convince a dead person to come alive again. The right alliances can create immeasurable access to even more alliances. From a variety of partnerships to having connections in different cultures, countries and those in different industries, every type of alliance serves as a conduit to helping you become a master of influence.

Partnerships

It's impossible for us to do everything on our own, even though most of us still try. This is why partnerships make a great solution to not only receiving help in areas where you need it most but they also increase your influence instantly by association. Any two or more entities coming together, combining resources to share and use to grow one another is a partnership. Several business partnerships are birthed when one business lacks in something that another can provide and vice versa. Working together, the possibilities become endless. In addition, the network of connections from both sides will often cross pollinate, expanding everyone involved. I'm often invited to sit on multiple for profit and nonprofit boards to provide my influence and expertise. In return, I receive access to their members, their network of contacts, potential business opportunities, plus the great reward of serving and helping others. Remain alert for fresh ideas to create new partnerships. As you begin to network on a larger scale, your influence alone can manifest partnership offers from every direction.

Cultural Alliances

Your alliances must, I repeat must, expand beyond your own race and culture. Being able to befriend, do business with or influence those from other cultures and those in different parts of the world is something you must pursue. To limit your influence is to waste your entire life. If you have no contacts or connections elsewhere around the world, then start connecting with people who do have them. There are several groups on professional social networks created strategically to bring cultures, nations and people together from all over. Join these, get involved in the discussions and while doing so, open the door for new contacts to come into your circle. You never know when you'll need someone from a different background, ethnicity or nationality to give you access or open a door to an opportunity that you couldn't open yourself. This is the power of cultural alliances. Learn about other cultures, their likes, dislikes, their foods, their capital cities and the people. If you're an entrepreneur, your cultural alliances can make you rich overnight. All it takes is one person in another country to create a brand new stream of income and a new set of followers that you never knew existed. Your influence can increase enormously from cultural alliances. You'll gain access into a privileged realm and experience something most people will never experience in their lifetime, and that something is globality.

Industry Alliances

There's nothing more detrimental to your influence than only having contacts and connections within your own industry of work or business. Thankfully I've been able to work in and venture into multiple industries such as entertainment, food & beverages, fashion, publishing, event services, real estate, professional training & coaching, hospitality and so on. The key to networking is very similar to investing, you need diversity. You never know when something will be a great success or a great failure, when something will start and how long before it ends, so you need options.

Industry alliances give you diversification to create more opportunities for yourself, just in case what you're working on doesn't work out. If you have future interests in other industries, it would be wise to start networking your way into those right now. I have industry alliances and connections in every industry known to man. That doesn't mean I do business with all of them, but I'm connected to them just in case I need a favor in some way or insight if I decide to enter that industry. You'd be amazed at how your influence can get you a lot of free stuff as well from industries you have nothing to do with. All I'm saying is, connect, connect, connect. It doesn't matter if it's the automotive industry, wine & spirits, textiles, aviation, entertainment, graphic design, oil

& energy or beauty products, diversify your contacts and your influence will be diversified. You can become an asset to all by being connected to all, making you one of the most powerful within your circle of influence.

Thoughts from Estonia

"Business is done between people, not between organisations. Networking and building strong relationships both online and offline is imperative for your success in business. In order to do business, you need to know people and efficient networking is what you should be doing on a regular basis, be it attending conferences or connecting with new contacts on Linkedin while having your morning coffee."

-Olesija Saue, Business Owner, Consultant

Success from Taiwan

"At Growth Hackers, we signed several partnerships with institutions, companies and agencies. This takes time and it doesn't happen overnight. Without networking, it would have been nearly impossible for us to build these strategic alliances."

-Jonathan Aufray, Co-founder and CEO at Growth Hackers

Advice from Bermuda

"In order to build long-term business alliances that are successful, you must first build trust and confidence. Have the right mindset and recognize that building a solid network of key connections will take time and effort but in the long run will produce long lasting dividends."

-Arthur Rego, President of AER Enterprises

LAW 7

GET ON THE GUEST LIST

Show others that they matter by getting involved with what they have going on. In return, they will encourage others to connect with you and also campaign for the world to follow you.

Creating, building and expanding your influence has a lot to do with name recognition and having a familiar face within circles of leaders and movers & shakers. Most of this is done simply by being in the right places, at the right time, as much as possible. Networkers network, they get out and meet other people. The world's most powerful also attend more than enough events. Your goal is to get on the guest list and join them whenever you can. Making contact in person builds trust much faster than a phone call or online. You should always show up when there's an opportunity to expand your influence amongst those who already have great influence. The familiarity of your face alone is enough to break the ice and grant you incredible access. Once you're in, you're in baby. The next time you're invited to an event, go, buy a ticket, Rsvp, whatever you have to do or contact the event producer and ask if they need any volunteers or additional help. This is how you get connected and stay connected.

Use this same strategy for charity functions, business seminars, award shows, golf tournaments, networking events, etc. As long as you keep your face and your name out there in the midst of it all, your influence will increase, it has no other choice. Getting on the guest list and showing up demonstrates devotion and dedication. The successful people I know never forget those that support them. They understand that people are the greatest asset to increase influence. Show others that they matter by getting involved with what they have going on. In return, they will encourage others to connect with you and also campaign for the world to follow you.

Thoughts from Croatia

"Networking is a basic ingredient of every opportunity discovery. Just essential."

-Goran Radic, Co-founder of Applicon, Applicon Tours, PandoPad, Payallo

Success from Barbados

"I met one of my mentors at a networking event and through that connection, I was able to implement his blueprint which led me to becoming the top producer on my team as well as hitting the top 5% within our company."

-Gavin Robinson, Entrepreneur

LAW 8

NETWORK EVERYWHERE

I believe every day of your life can present opportunities to network. We may not be conscious of it but it's there. We may not exchange contact information each time or start negotiations on the spot, but we're still networking indirectly. Take for example, you're in a department store and a store clerk walks up to assist you. At that exact moment a door opens to network. You may have a nephew or friend in need of a job, so you ask the clerk if they are currently hiring. Regardless if the answer is yes or no, you've made a connection with someone that could potentially open a door for present or future opportunities and possibilities, which is exactly what networking is all about.

In restaurants, when you leave a tip or even if you decide not to, you should leave your business card. At parties or gatherings, offer to bring an item or give away a gift, courtesy of your business. There are endless networking opportunities awaiting us every single day, in a cab, at work, at the gym or a party, at church, in traffic, on an airplane, wherever the opportunity presents itself, you should network. Success is much closer than most people realize. It is the fear of risk that makes it seem so far away. When we truly utilize the power of networking and the unlimited resources and assistance it can bring into your life, we formulate an atmosphere to become rich in all aspects, not just money, but also rich in joy, health, family, friends and the desire within us to help others succeed.

Thoughts from Australia

"Networking on any level opens doorways to opportunities and helps you gain recognition, confidence and self-worth."

-Tez Blackmore, Business Development Director

Advice from Czech Republic

"Present yourself, wherever you can and do as many one on one meetings as possible."

-Gabriel Szalay, Founder Tickle It

LAW 9

PUT YOUR NETWORK TO WORK

What's the purpose of having thousands of business contacts on a professional social network and not knowing how to or not being able to utilize them for something? It's a waste, a huge waste. You should delete your profile right now or start interacting with your network to make something happen. We're all busy, you're not the only one, so don't ever use that excuse again. Your credibility is built by people actually knowing what you are about, which means sooner or later you'll need to interact with someone. You can do this in a variety of ways, starting by just responding positively to a few posts or discussions from your contacts online. If it's something you like, something that resonates with you, your beliefs and so forth, thank them for posting it. You'd be surprised how you'll quickly jump from a contact to a friend when you support your connections with encouraging responses. If you desire to take things up a notch, host a free holiday networking party at your home or somewhere central. It doesn't hurt to spend a few bucks on food and beverages to get to know people who could expand your life. Trust me it's worth it, I've done it and look at me now. You can save money by getting other people involved and asking them to bring or buy a designated item for the event. Make it a networking power party!

For those who desire something more public and less intimate, invite some of your contacts to go bowling. Those of you who are big sports fans can buy a few extra game tickets and invite some of your most powerful connections in your area to attend with you, your treat. Not many people will turn down a free game night out, that's for sure. There are several creative ways to prepare your network to do exactly what they were meant to do, be an asset to you, and vice versa. More than likely, each person in your network is connected to someone who can either benefit from knowing you or open a door of opportunity for you. Everyone in your network should be quick to promote or refer you when they come across something that brings you to mind. This is putting your network to work for you. You should be doing the same for them as well. Get to know those who you need to know, so they can help you achieve what you desire to achieve. Use whatever strategies necessary to put your network to work.

Thoughts from Malta

"Networking is important because eventually you create a web of potential leads that in turn create work and prosperity for both yourself and a number of other people within your network. You will also have several opportunities to increase your brand or visibility through the many other networks, people in your network are affiliated to."

-Brian Role', Magician & Illusionist

Success from Israel

"Building a network of incredible friends, colleagues and professional contacts helped me build a major media trade association (aka: a lobby) in Washington, DC."

-Yasha Harari, SEO Fiverr

Wealth.

Wealth can be measured by currency, by lives positively impacted by yours, and by peace of mind. True wealth combines all three. Accumulation of them all should be your desire. You can have one without the other two and still have some success, this is possible. You can also have two of the three as well, which is much better than just one. Great ideas and multiple streams of income can create riches in currency. Wealth arrives when your presence alone pays for everything, and you can leave your wallet at home. Motivating and empowering others makes you a great inspiration. Wealth arrives when they take what you've taught them and teach it to someone else, duplicating this cycle for generations. Networking easily grants you access to the first two measurements of wealth but peace of mind is only given by God. As you obtain all three, you will be offered wealth in all aspects of life plus potentially unlimited territorial access around the world.

LAW 10

ASK GOD FOR IDEAS

Ideas are forever present, all around us, every single day, swimming freely in this immeasurable creative atmosphere of existence.

I am a firm believer that God is the originator of ideas. You can believe whatever you desire, I have no problem with that, but as for me, He gives me my ideas. There are so many others, including some of our greatest inventors, world renowned entrepreneurs, and leaders who have confessed the same. Look around you, wherever you are, what do you see? Everything in view was someone else's idea. The physical book you're reading in your hand or the digital screen you're reading it on, was an idea. Our clothes we have on, the cars we drive, the beds we sleep in, the tv's we watch, the phones we talk and text on, all ideas. If you want influence, wealth and power, an idea is a sure way to obtain it all. You can invest in the stock market and every other market for a lifetime and still die broke. If you want to play ball with the biggest movers & shakers of the world, grab a great idea and then head to the networking playing field. I believe we receive ideas in three ways; by influence, inheritance and impartation.

Ideas by Influence

You'd be surprised how everyday life, circumstances and people can influence your next idea. It does take a certain amount of observation to receive ideas by influence. Several of the greatest ideas of our generation were derived this way. These include inventions, products and services that were most likely influenced by a need or desire. Other ideas include the innovation of a current idea to make it better, easier, stronger, faster, more efficient, or safer. For ideas by influence, you could be at home, out with friends at a restaurant, at work, traveling, shopping, anywhere at any moment, and receive an idea from your surroundings or experience at that time. Ideas are forever present, all around us, every single day, swimming freely in this immeasurable creative atmosphere of existence.

Ideas by Inheritance

Some families are just really, really lucky, blessed beyond measure. Generation to generation, they seem to soar in just about everything they do, especially in ideas. There are global dynasties, last names that will never be forgotten, with heirs who only continue to expand on what was established before them by their grandparents, parents or other family members. Ideas can be genetic, rooted in our ancestry. A family of idea generators, entrepreneurs, philanthropists, business owners and self-starters usually produces more of the same, so it's not uncommon. Sometimes a thorough research of our ancestry can open up a book of ideas we never knew existed. Your next level of influence could be waiting for the motivation from what you discover. We all have a history, great people have walked before us. Often, knowing that history is exactly what we need to position ourselves for future success that supersedes all of those prior.

Ideas by Impartation

In many confirmed cases and definitely in mine, ideas are imparted through a vision, a dream or instantly dropped into your spirit at any given moment from God. I love when this happens and I believe the more ideas you ask for, the more you'll receive. Many inventors and even some scientists have attested to some type of divine impartation for their inventions and discoveries, acknowledging a supernatural guidance or enlightenment. I'm a firm believer that the Earth is a sacred realm, and that no disease can enter this realm without first the cure already being here. I believe the cure to every disease may not be discovered by research, yet instead, by impartation from a higher source.

All of my book ideas come to me through divine impartation. I find myself constantly asking God for more and more ideas. Each time I receive one and act upon it, no matter how long it takes to implement it, my life is promoted to another level. Now don't go assuming everything that pops into your head is an idea by impartation, most likely it isn't. These ideas are strategic, filled with unbelievable passion, and all arriving with a higher purpose. Whether by influence, inheritance, or impartation, all ideas have the power to make you more valuable, more influential, and richer. The objective of ideas is to expand your life and/or the world around you. Pay attention to your ideas and your ideas will pay you for life.

Thoughts from Greece

"You can expose your ideas and get exposed to the ideas of people you could never meet or know in any other case. In addition, you have a solid basis to launch new ideas."

-Socratis Ploussas, CEO Mellon advisory Ltd

Advice from Albania

"You need to take networking into the real world, where it's needed most, not only in the virtual world."

-Armando Shkurti, Android Developer

LAW 11
ACTIVATE YOUR IMAGINATION

Let observation and awareness carry a bright torch everywhere you go, providing a lifetime of light by which your imagination can be led and then used to lead.

Take heed to your creative thoughts, no matter how random or outrageous they may seem. Your imagination can create a brand new world. Most people are so preoccupied until they can't have even one creative thought a day, but you must be the exception. Your wealth depends on it. Imagination has something to do with every creation and invention. Imagination also advances your networking by helping both parties create mutual benefits. Do not silence your imagination. Instead, feed it and nurture it. Let observation and awareness carry a bright torch everywhere you go, providing a lifetime of light by which your imagination can be led and then used to lead.

Thoughts from United Kingdom
"Life and business happens thanks to people. The more and better you know through networking, the easier life will be."
-Yannis Karipsiadis, CEO

Success from Cameroon
"Through networking with various leaders and entrepreneurs, I made the decision to become an entrepreneur."
-Ndel-Andre Raoul, Head of Marketing, Sales and Business Development

GERMAINE MOODY

LAW 12
SURROUND YOURSELF WITH GENIUSES

Networking is not just to connect with those of like passions and interests. Networking is for treading into unknown waters, discovering fresh ideas, possessing new lands, and experiencing the unlimited.

Wealthy people have wealthy friends. Smart people have smart friends. Ignorant people have ignorant friends. If you desire to be smart and wealthy, you should start befriending individuals that fall into those categories and circles. I've made it mandatory to surround myself with people who know more than I do, those that have greater wisdom or insight about everything that I have little to no knowledge of. If I want to learn more about the oil & energy industry, I befriend professionals in that field, and the same goes for anything else. A sure way to expand your education, your opportunities, your global connections, and your own ideas, is to surround yourself with geniuses, those who know what you desire to learn. You should always hold open an door for expansion, to learn something new. Power networking connects you to everyone, from every walk of life, every industry, and in every country that you can possibly connect to. There are people all over the world who will mentor you for free if you just ask. The potential to create or multiply wealth also increases each time you connect with someone outside of your own field of interest or industry, so don't limit yourself. Networking is not just to connect with those of like passions and interests. Networking is for treading into unknown waters, discovering fresh ideas, possessing new lands, and experiencing the unlimited.

Thoughts from Ireland

"Networking creates an avenue for people in diverse businesses, skills and professions to grow. It brings a global world together and forms a close knit community of skilled individuals, sharing ideas while also creating a chain where knowledge is shared."

-Ogbeyalu Okoye, Forensic Accountant,
Risk and Financial Analyst

Advice from Dominican Republic

"Help fellow networkers as much as you can. Focus on quality of relationships, not quantity. Don't try to take advantage of others. Learn from the more experienced. Always offer something valuable."

-Edison Sepúlveda, Consultant

LAW 13
PRODUCE. PRODUCE. PRODUCE.

You have the ideas, you're surrounded by those who can help turn your ideas into reality, now it's time to produce. Unless you inherit your fortune, you will mostly likely need to produce something in order to enter the circle of wealth. What you produce or what you are capable of producing is the dish that you bring to the networking table. Tap into what comes natural for you, your gifts, talents, skills, knowledge about certain things. Use this to create a product or service and then monetize it. Whatever it is you do best that others value, you can make money from. Do it consecutively and become the best at it.

There are brands that have been around for ages because they continue to produce nonstop. There are singers, authors, investors, business professionals and public figures who have made fortunes because they continue to produce and evolve. If you produce nothing, you will gain nothing. The biggest movers & shakers want to network with those who have produced something. Even if you only produce a great idea to share with them, that's a start, as ideas provide the fuel used to drive the world's richest. Not everyone is an inventor, and the majority of the world's population will never be entrepreneurs, but I tell you this and listen closely, the greatest road to becoming and remaining wealthy is by paving it for yourself. This can only be done by hiring yourself, investing in yourself, working for yourself, and then creating, producing and operating on a level unmatched by those around you.

Thoughts from Nigeria

"As a business owner I run my new business ideas through my network (thereby cutting down the money on hiring a research company), once a product or service is developed I run a sample via my network to determine the acceptability. After product development, I introduce the product/service to my network who make-up my first line of buyers and their referrals help my business to grow."

-Olushola Olaleye, CEO, Payers and Pledge Entertainment Limited

Success from Denmark

"Through networking, I met a guy filled with grief and stress, but he had promised his best friend, his dog Charlie, that never again should a dog die from bad feed. He wanted revenge on producers. In the year that followed, we helped him with product and business development, I had daily conversations with him. He developed a great product, top quality at a reasonable price, all starting with an investment of 1,500 euros. It received a super positive response and sales increased. As it happened, the factory that produced his feed went on sale, so his network helped him find two investors. And a year after starting his brand, he and two others took over the plant with 25 employees. He is now two years later, due to hard work and continual networking, exporting to six countries and still growing."

-Lynge Hansen, Country Manager

LAW 14

MARKET YOURSELF OR BE IGNORED

People are searching for hope, excitement and leadership daily, give it to them and they'll be eating out your hands.

Knowing who you are, what you're about, and how to present that to the world, is the most important thing in the game of networking. It could make the difference between a $10,000 deal and a $10,000,000 deal. First and foremost, it's important that you discover the things that set you apart from the rest. This should always be used to your advantage. Status quo people often associate with status quo people, secretly desiring to be amongst the power players. Secondly, you need to know what you want and to what degree or amount you want it. How much success, how much influence, how much money, how much power, how much access? Knowing these answers will help you decide on the levels and best ways to market yourself and create some noise, plus keep you alert to opportunities from others that line up with your master plan.

Master Marketing Yourself:
Words, Image & Personality

No one should know you better than you. If someone else does, then you're in trouble. You can hire a publicist, a manager, an agent, and whoever else but you better know the person in the mirror before you do that. You don't want to become something that you can't live up to behind closed doors. Just watch the news nightly and you'll see many of these scenarios. To master marketing yourself, you should start with mastering words (Law #1). When communicating one on one, face to face in-person or on the telephone, marketing online and in the media, or if you're out in public, use words that create an emotional response with people, those that show respect, camaraderie, joy, humility, hope, strength, passion and elation. People are searching for hope, excitement and leadership daily, give it to them and they'll be eating out of your hands. Words and phrases like "together", "mutually beneficial", "I consider this a privilege", "we", "amazing", "awesome", "I'm beyond excited", "phenomenal", "exclusive", "You're amazing", "unprecedented", "life-changing", "everything is possible", are just a few of the ones I use when communicating, marketing and networking.

Image

Your physical image plays a mighty role as well. How you appear means everything in networking, well, at least until you become filthy rich, but until then do whatever it takes to keep yourself looking up to par or above par. Everything is about perception in networking and in today's world. If you appear a certain way, most people will believe you are that way.

Personality

Your personality is the most important asset when marketing yourself, especially in the case of making new connections. It should definitely influence your marketing ideas and strategies. When making an introduction to new potential contacts, keep it short, direct, intriguing, full of your unique personality, with a side of excitement and to the point. The average person's attention span is shorter than your thumb. Boring people create boring marketing, and boring marketing puts people to sleep and out of business. Your goal is to generate interest and get a response, so let your personality shine through.

Sample Introduction Emails For Networking

Below are two sample emails you can use when first contacting a new person to add to your network. You can customize them to fit your personality so that it sounds authentic but I suggest using as much of the sample as possible. If you don't have a personality, you need to work on creating one. The greatest networkers are excited, observant, supportive and optimistic people.

Sample #1

Greetings John, *(I use the person's first name, but use what makes you comfortable)*

My name is Jane Doe (replace with your name), and I want to first thank you for the amazing work you do as a teacher and leader (list their job/career, specialty, organization, charity work, etc). I'm inspired by your dedication, expertise and passion. Currently I work in banking and I'm a youth motivational speaker. I make it a point to surround myself with great individuals such as yourself so that I'm able to grow and expand. It would be an honor to connect with you as a new colleague and friend. If there's any synergy for us to create, collaborate, build or offer mutual support, I'm all in. Thanks again John!

Sincerely,
Jane Doe

With the sample above, you'll rarely be denied a new connection and you'll get a response in most cases if the person is not exceptionally busy. This next sample has more of a risk to it because it can be perceived as extreme. Some people aren't as motivated and excited as others, so you may be ignored by a few people that receive the following one, but that's fine, who wants boring contacts anyway? I sure don't. It's always good to study the other person's profile first and then decide which one to use.

Sample #2

John!

You're awesome! Thank you for everything you do and for sharing your genius with the world. Just by reading your profile I can tell that you're someone I could learn a lot from and that I would love to have in my circle of greatness. It's rare to find genuinely positive and big thinking individuals like yourself. I'd like to add you to my network and be a part of yours as well. If I can assist you in any way, let me know, and if there's a possibility for us to work together or create, I'm open to all suggestions. Looking forward to the unlimited possibilities!

Rock the week!
Jane Doe

The second sample will attract the serial networker rockstars, they totally understand where you're coming from. On the other hand, the scrooges won't reply, or they'll just add you without responding. Both are great to use, depending on who you're contacting. It's hard not to reply to someone who exudes energy, enthusiasm and also praises you at the same time. You want to connect with as many life-giving professionals as possible. These are the ones that will enhance your networking and help expand your circle tremendously.

What Not To Include In Your Introduction Message

A sure way to sabotage new connections and future connections is to not know how to properly introduce yourself. There are several scenarios that you need to stay away from. Here's a list of what not to do when reaching out to new connections for the first time.

1. **Don't tell your life story with a long introduction.** Your greeting should be friendly, to the point and by all means brief. You are making an introduction only, not a biopic. I prefer no more than five to seven sentences when people initially reach out to me and introduce themselves.

2. **Don't present a "paid" opportunity to people in your initial message to them.** Most people will not pay you $399 to start a home-based business to supplement their income when they have no idea of who the hell you are. There is a process to warming up to new connections and clients. Build the communication and trust first if you want people to eventually hear about any opportunity. Being referred to them by a mutual connection and mentioning that person's name will build trust faster and help break down introduction barriers.

3. **Don't ask how much money someone makes, how much their company makes or inquire about their net worth.** Believe it or not, people do this. When introducing yourself to someone for the first time, don't ask them about their personal or business finances. On the other hand, if someone contacts you with an opportunity, say to join a company, become an affiliate or something of that nature, then it's fine for you to reply and ask them how much money they've made with that opportunity themselves.

4. **Don't ask for someone's phone number in your initial message to them.** You are taking a huge risk by asking someone for their contact number in your first message to them. I recommend that you don't do this. It can come off as desperate and scary to some, depending on who you're contacting. If you desire to share information or include someone on something, it's best to state what that something is first, and see if they are interested. Asking for their number may get you an offensive response, no response at all or even blocked. I'm not saying it won't work in your favor with some, but for others, it can backfire and cause you to lose a potential connection instantly.

5. **Don't tell someone to call you about an opportunity.** This has been happening a lot more frequently. People are getting desperate. Refrain from your first message telling someone to call you for information about a big opportunity. It's a complete turn off and raises several red flags. Your introduction needs to be less questionable if you want to gain resourceful and respectable connections. Stick to the basics in your introduction message. Furthermore, if you can't send a brief summary of an opportunity without sending five videos and ten website links to view, then you're in the wrong business friend.

6. **Don't ask people "What do you do?" when it's obvious on their profile page.** If someone mentions their companies, current job positions, expertise, passions and pursuits, skills, mission, life purpose, accomplishments, and specialties on their profile, please read them. Asking them "What do you do?" will only show that you are clueless to who you are messaging. This poses a question of your professionalism and attentiveness. In your

introduction message you need to mention something significant about them that you read prior to contacting them. This always impresses the new connection and has a very high response rate.

Thoughts from France

"Breathing, Networking, Marketing... all describe mandatory activities ensuring our very survival as individuals and the survival of our business. It's a fact, if we fail to breathe we die within minutes, networking and marketing are like our left and right lungs in the business world. If we fail at networking and marketing our business properly, we soon end up in front of a bankruptcy court so it's not a question of whether we should do it or not but rather how we should do it."

-Christophe Poizat, Partner, Global Ocean Plastic Waste Recovery Program

Advice from Finland

"Personal activity is always important, and open-mindedness. Focus upon creating your personal brand and focus on content. High quality will be rewarded with many followers and future possibilities and opportunities. Use common sense also, both online and offline."

-Anne-Maria Yritys, Creative Director at Y.E.S./Yritys Executive Services

GERMAINE MOODY

LAW 15
YOU ARE A BRAND

Branding is about possessing territory, having your own place in the world, in the lives of consumers and followers.

Marketing makes you rich. Branding makes you wealthy. When it comes to networking, you will become a personal brand, whether you want to or not. Networking connects you with a variety of people, who are also brands, though some may not look at it that way, but you should. The more you connect with successful people who are also successful personal brands, the bigger your brand becomes. Your online profiles should be clear about who you are, what you're about, what you're doing, what you support, and what you desire to achieve. Clarity is essential in order for you to connect with movers & shakers. The most powerful and most influential people won't spend a lot time trying to figure you out by emailing you a variety of questions to understand your personal brand. Your brand should be spelled out and obvious. Networking systemically grows your personal brand when your contacts share or mention you to their contacts and followers, instantly expanding your influence and access. Understanding that you are a brand is vital. Your networking will amount to zero if your personal brand isn't clear and visible.

Brand Yourself

Branding yourself is to identify what differentiates you from everyone else, then successfully communicating that to those you desire to know. What do you offer, what do you stand for, who are you, what's unique about you, your product, your service, your purpose? Focus on what makes you or your company great. The secret to branding lies in becoming embedded into the minds and hearts of customers, constituents, followers, the masses, the world. Several public figures and some of the largest corporations accomplish this by creating long-term emotional connections with their audience or customers. Words lead the pack for generating emotional responses from most people, this is why mastering words is so important from the start.

People rarely remember anything that wasn't different or that didn't stand out. When they think of you or your company, your personal brand should automatically give them some sense of what to expect. The stronger and clearer your brand, the better. You don't need tons of money to brand yourself, but you do need to know who you are and what's your overall message. Whatever you bring to the table through your personal brand, perfect it and market it as the only solution needed. Branding is about possessing territory, having your own place in the world, in the lives of consumers and followers. As you are establishing your personal brand, use networking to magnify it and to create more opportunities for additional income streams.

Increase Your Globality & Income

An incredible benefit of networking is that people will market you and promote your brand for free. I know professionals who are known globally but have never spent a dime on marketing, advertising, or promotion. It's all been done through networking. They've established their brands online and that alone has drawn others to them. Their work, their personality, their fundamental beliefs, their mission, and their purpose have all been used to form their brand. Your networking should be strategic and you should have a thought-out plan as to the regions and locations around the world where you want your brand to flourish. This way your contacts who have connections in those regions will know who to recommend or suggest to you when they come across something that fits your vision. If you want to instantly expand your product, service, career, mission or your personal brand into another country, start networking with others in those countries right away.

The more people/personal brands you connect with, the more chances for success and new opportunities you will receive. This is cross-branding in networking, when two entities connect and each adds value to the other, expanding brand reach and marketability. Let your connections help market your brand. This gives you automatic credibility plus association with their brand, which can create a whole new set of loyal followers, customers and supporters. Your marketing strategies can change but your overall personal brand message should remain intact. Personal brands that motivate, inspire, create positive change, and innovate are normally the ones that stand out the most. This is because of the lack of hope portrayed in the media around the world. Instead of daily positive news, we're inundated with negative stories full of drama, poverty and dismay. If you give people hope, a reason to continue, something to make them feel better about being alive while living a life of uncertainty day to day, they will give you their attention, support and money. Public figures, motivational speakers and several celebrities have launched global revivals of hope and positivity, and in return the world gives them millions and billions of dollars because of it. Religion also produces hope, and the money flows nonstop. Whether it's hope or something else, your life must line up with your brand. Be authentic. Master who you are, your brand, and people will follow, so will the money.

Thoughts from Bolivia

"Our world has changed and we just don't limit ourselves to the city or country we live in, the internet allows us to connect worldwide. For every activity we perform, we must consider our worldwide audience. In these days we need to speak to the millions of people out there, networking is the fundamental part of this process."

-Carla Doria-Medina, Technical Writer

Success from Philippines

"Because of networking with eminent credible scholars in both local and international arena, I have been recommended globally as speaker, lecturer/professor, facilitator, session academic chair, etc. I have also been referred or recommended for international leaderships e.g as member of the Scientific Board (Europe, USA, Australia, and Asia) and as a recipient of several prestigious awards."

-Angelica M. Baylon, Exec. Director of the Maritime Academy of Asia and the Pacific

LAW 16
MASTER NEGOTIATING

Your ultimate level of wealth will come down to negotiating. Being able to negotiate, to master negotiating, is what eventually separates the powerful from the powerless. If you don't believe you're any good at negotiating, find someone to do it on your behalf. Bad negotiations lead to destruction and poverty. Here are four steps to help you negotiate successfully and to turn networking opportunities into something much larger than what was originally intended.

Analyze The Player And The Playing Field

The first thing you need to know is who you're dealing with, meaning do your research on the person or entity that you're about to enter a business deal or negotiations with. Having some background information on how they operate or like to work gives you an advantage. If this person is known to be aggressive and likes to get straight to the point, prepare yourself to do the same. Most professionals migrate to other professionals who are similar to them or who they esteem greater when it comes to doing business. It's the same with networking. After a while, people develop patterns, so anything you can learn about them prior will benefit you. Find something positive about the person before you get on a phone call or meet in person. People are flattered and impressed when you mention something good about them. Get as much of a grip on who they are, their likes, dislikes, mission, connections or inner circle, then you can easily lead them into eating out of the palm of your hands. Take notes, research enough so that you feel confident and prepared.

Analyze The Offer

Secondly, get a full understanding of the deal at hand by analyzing the offer. Make sure you know what is being presented and how each party is planning to benefit. Is it worth entering into? Is it great for making a lot of money or is a great cross-marketing opportunity? Will being a part of this deal increase your credibility or influence? Are there additional opportunities that can come about from it? Does the deal make sense? Is it a short-term or long-term deal? You need to be able to answer all of these questions so that you can strategically prepare and present your contribution in the deal.

Analyze The Player's Contribution

Next, you need to know what the other person or entity is bringing to the table. If you can, always let them disclose their contribution to the deal first, that way you're able to then come back with your contribution and deliver more if necessary to have the upper hand. Having the upper hand gives you more clout and allows you to request more in the negotiation process. It doesn't work that way all the time but in most cases the biggest contributor in a deal gets the greatest benefit or percentage. On the other hand, sometimes it's good to just simplify negotiations on a 50/50 basis, calling it even.

Assess. Add. Ask.

Now that you've analyzed the player, the playing field, the offer, and their contribution, it's time to Assess the entire situation so you can offer up your contribution in the negotiation. If you know that your contribution includes more work, more hours, or has more of a substantial impact on the overall deal, then be sure to bring this to the table. Now Add your contribution, let them know what you can do and will do as a part of this deal. If you feel that both parties bring an equal amount of value, then it's best to equally share everything as far as the benefits, profits and so on. If you bring undeniably more to the table, then don't be afraid to Ask for more from the deal. Always remain open to hear their side while staying prepared to defend and explain why you should receive more if that's the case. Keeping everything peaceful of course, most seasoned professionals will already know who deserves this and that in negotiations, or whether to split everything even.

Thoughts from Saint Vincent And The Grenadines
"Networking is an essential undercurrent of any industry, it's the circuit that connects people of like minds and vocation to share information, experiences, best practices and innovations. Without this lifeline, the root of cooperation would decay, the branches of capitalism will wither and the fruits of fortune 100 companies will cease to exist."
-Hayden Billingy, CEO of Hayden Billingy Music

Advice from Lesotho
"Networking is essential for the success of any business. Most of the long-term clients you will have will be as a result of your ability to interact with people. The key to networking is to never turn it off. Your every encounter should leave you and the other person having learnt something from each other. Talking about you or your business does not have to be an all evening event, pick five sentences that will leave a lasting impression about you and your business. Every opportunity to network is an opportunity to sway minds your way, so take it. Know what is happening around you (current affairs, news), that way you will have things to talk about other than your business."
-Ma-Lord T Mefane, Managing Director
Mankabelane Communications

GERMAINE MOODY

LAW 17
SLEEP WHEN YOU'RE DEAD OR RICH

Too much sleep can become your biggest opposition to wealth. Indeed we all need proper rest but discovering just how much you need and don't need in order to operate at high levels of productivity and creativity is the key. I've had issues with not getting enough sleep in the past, as millions do daily, and the main reason for myself and others is due to distractions or plain lack of discipline. If you plan to accumulate great wealth and be successful at it, you will have to adjust your life to your mission. Most nights I'm in bed by 7pm or no later than 8pm. Going to bed much earlier than the majority of the world and waking up before them allows you quiet time to exhale. If you study millionaires and billionaires, most will advocate the importance of early morning hours to read, study, exercise. meditate, pray, or work more to stay ahead of the rest. If you're a global networker, you should also use those early morning hours to communicate or do business with other parts of the world while they are awake.

Until you reach your goals in life, sleep should only be used to get enough rest for work and to stay healthy. Other than that, you need to be up seven days a week, networking, producing and working your way to where you desire to be. Millions if not billions of people sleep their lives away, never reaching their goals, let alone becoming wealthy. Spending more time awake brainstorming your wealth strategy and networking with others doing the same, will fast forward your results. The majority of people only make money when they're awake, only a few make money in their sleep. Let that be your new motivation when you awake, to create additional income streams that allow you to build wealth while you're counting sheep. It is important that you become rich. Your life can impact more people and help more people when you do. Begin networking with those who feel the same way about this as you do, and in common hours you'll begin to encounter new levels of abundance in multiple areas of life.

Thoughts from Montserrat
"Success is not the effort of the sole individual. It is a combination of one's efforts, tenacity and contacts. Your net worth is really largely dependent on your network!"
-*Warren Cassell, Entertainment Attorney and Author*

Success from Gibraltar
"I am thankful for the opportunities I have had in working at various law firms over the Summer. As a result I have met many lawyers and if you want to get into a career in law, apart from good grades, people need to know you as a person and a professional. I have a few interviews over the Summer after I finish Bar school because I went out of my way to network; I met people and was genuinely interested in developing relationships, beyond small talk."
-*Daniel Bula, Bar Student*

LAW 18
EMBRACE GLOBAL CURRENCIES

There's not enough money in America. There's not enough money in Europe. There is not enough money in Australia. I think you get the point. Discovering global currencies, ways how to accumulate more of them, and networking with people in countries where their currency is remarkably beneficial to yours is an additional way to grow wealth. Conversion rates can make a significant difference and instantly multiply the value of the money you have in other countries. It's best to know as much as possible pertaining to currencies because when you network, new territories will eventually open, and your knowledge and awareness are crucial to do business or negotiate when called upon. My advice is to keep abreast of the top 7 currencies in the world, then strategically connect with other entrepreneurs, business professionals and opportunities in those regions. There's nothing wrong with growing your money and using other currencies and countries to do so, the rich do it all the time. Wealth should be watched and followed. Don't waste time trying to figure it all out on your own. Follow those who have done it already and continue to do it. Go straight to the top, and don't be afraid to ask questions. Network globally, become wealthy worldwide.

Thoughts from Hong Kong
"The modern Internet has created a world of complete connectivity. In the next 5-10 years we expect to see much of the rest of the world's population come online. How then, do we stand out in this world of infinite noise? We do so by networking. The

connections you make on this journey we call life are critical to our survival in both our professional and our personal lives."
-*Jay Kim, Host of The Jay Kim Show*

Success from Suriname

"I am the founder of Inspiring Ladies of Color Speaking events and because of my international network and my networking skills, I am able to organize events internationally and find the best people to work with me on making the events a huge success."
-*Ruth Sinkeler, Owner of CLIP Training & Consultancy*

Advice from Cote D'Ivoire

"Treat each other like partners, friends, collaborators and not like an enemy. Use your differences to build a strong network in terms of cultural collaboration."
-*Toti Jean Marc Yale, Nonprofit Founder*

LAW 19
GET YOUR B.S. TOGETHER

We all know what "BS" means in the real world but for now it means Billionaire Squad. Why are there so few billionaires? Because people don't have their teams and squads together. Most people would rather get together to go see a movie, ride out for a drink, attend a sports game, or have a 3rd family reunion within the same year with a bunch of broke relatives asking each other for money. Get your BS together! Instead of the five of you spending over $100 to watch a movie about rich people, take that $100 and go lock yourself in a hotel room for 24 hours and brainstorm the next billion dollar idea. Who does that? Nobody. And that's why the 1% remains the 1%. If you think like the 99%, you will remain in it. Everywhere you look there's a business conference, convention, seminar and so on. If you were to take 200 attendees at a business conference and only discuss ideas to create a new multi-billion dollar company, I guarantee you, someone if not everyone in that group will become rich. Now is the time to surround yourself with like-minded people, full of curiosity and determination. The more you network, the more of them you'll meet. People have complained for years about their families not supporting them. For the record, you don't need your family's support. It would be great to have but you can't wait on a dead horse to giddy up. What you need is your Billionaire Squad, those who desire to join forces with you to achieve what most people only dream about.

How do you find your BS Squad? You must first be aware of what you want to accomplish. How many people do you desire to help as a philanthropist and in what parts of your country or the world? How much money do you want to make? Define your goals and let those define who you seek to connect with. Ultimately, you want to keep the doors open because you never know who will know someone that you need to know. By all means network strategically, your BS Squad is literally waiting on you. Some are living unfulfilled lives because they were born to play a major part in yours. Find your billionaire squad, tell them the wait is over, and get to work.

Thoughts from Bosnia And Herzegovina

"Networking is not a luxury but rather a necessity. If you want to be successful, you can't do it alone. You are as strong as your network."

-Selma Sehic, Community Manager UP Sarajevo

Success from Zambia

"Through my network I was able to create and sustain my business. Before I started I had no idea how to put certain things in place and how to implement certain strategy. With a background in engineering, my exposure to business and wealth creation was not as apparent as white collar job exposure. When I started my business, it would have taken decades to move from very low income growth to relatively high income sustainability, but with seasoned business men and technology mentor in my network, it was easier to grow at a faster rate than it would take most people to grow."

-Mutoba Ngoma, CEO Tapera Industries Limited

Power.

The greatest power is to lead and have others follow you. The greatest power is to speak and have others listen. The greatest power is to go against the status quo because it only makes sense to the majority. Power in life cannot be summed up easily. There are several realms of power, some dark and others full of light. It is demonstrated in multiple situations throughout each day. Networking is a great friend and respecter of power, for each time you connect to another person, your power increases. Power is deadly and it gives birth. It is a game and it is real life. It can provide freedom and captivity. It produces peace and destruction. Not knowing the power you can gain from networking, and not knowing the power you already have, is equally dangerous as the misuse of it.

LAW 20

SELF-AWARENESS IS YOUR GREATEST POWER

Power. What is it? How do you obtain it? What power do you already have? Power cannot be summed up easily but the greatest power you'll ever have access to in your lifetime is the power of self-awareness. You will amount to nothing if you aren't mindful of yourself. This awareness helps you to discover and pursue all that is great and best for you, while encouraging you to expect the same from those that come into your life. Self-awareness is obtained through solitude, observation, and evaluation. **Solitude** requires you to spend time alone, getting to know yourself, and understanding your own thought processes. Too many outside voices create confusion and double-mindedness. **Observation** provides a wealth of knowledge about what you must contribute to the world in your lifetime. **Self-evaluation** shines an inner light on your past decisions, present pursuits and future growth, helping you determine the next best move and the perfect timing. One must master self-awareness to truly master networking. You'll end up wasting your energy with the wrong people if you don't. Your goal should be to become a master of networking, for in becoming a master of networking, you become a master of people. And when you become a master of people, you will always be the most powerful person in the room.

Thoughts from China

"Networking and communication have always been important elements for business, friendship and daily life, whether in the old days or right now in this digital century. Fundamentally, we need to make sure the world understands who we are, what we have and don't have, what we intend to achieve, what we expect from one another, our feelings and passion, our fears and tears and vice versa. For business and work, we ought to be in front of people through face to face meetings, messaging, voice and video sessions to understand each other and learn about opportunities, options and detect potential risks. Without networking, no consolidation power, we can hardly achieve any objective."

-Andrew S. Cheung, Founding Partner and Advisor

Advice from Argentina

"Be honest. Be true. Be yourself. Don't spam. Don't cheat. Don't underestimate."

-Rodrigo Borgia, CEO Gamifica

LAW 21

THE LAW OF W.A.L.E.S.

Finding common ground and necessity is an asset to worldwide networking and an invitation to global power.

Knowledge and communication are two giant assets to gaining power. Knowledge is able to place you before the world's most influential and affluent, including the one percent of the 1%. Great communication skills are capable of convincing your biggest critics and doubters. Combined, these two can guide you into unlimited realms of perpetual power. There are five mandatory keys to mastering them both, I call them "The Law of W.A.L.E.S." (Watch, Ask, Listen, Exchange, Study).

Watch

Besides money and influence, which are huge gatekeepers to power, information is by far the least expensive way to gain power. The Law of WALES helps you obtain that power through observation, starting with the ability to Watch. There is an unprecedented amount of access nowadays to everything going on, anywhere and at any time. You can watch people, countries, cultures, events, it's all available on a global scale. The more observant you are, the more knowledge you will accumulate, and this increases your value when networking. The most successful people in the world desire to connect with those who have vast knowledge in areas that they don't. It is at this point when you must realize that watching has great monetary value. By watching, you can learn how to communicate with masses of people and connect in different levels of society, which automatically expands your network. The greater your network, the greater your value. When in this realm of power, people will pay you just to be connected to you. This law, to Watch, is also consistently in a state of self-awareness mentally and spiritually, not just physically. To know where you are and what you are surrounded by, seen and unseen, will propel you to your higher self, and people will flock to network with you and support all that you do.

Ask

Ask and you shall receive. Those five words may sound cliché but they contain the keys to getting exactly what you want in life. It takes boldness to ask. It takes aggressiveness to ask. Even when connecting and networking with others, you are asking to enter another person's circle of influence. Once in, and after you get a feel for the individual, ask how you can be of assistance to help them achieve their goals and pursuits. Anytime you're the first to offer assistance in networking, you establish an immediate bond and appreciation with the other person, which gives you permission down the line to ask for something in return later. Using this technique over and over will increase your power and allies.

As for knowledge and information you need to know, ask as many questions as possible to get your answers. Never go to bed not knowing. Some people let their pride keep them ignorant, which ultimately results in poverty. Don't try to wing it in a conversation, pretending you know something when you really don't. Most professionals love talking about themselves and answering great questions, it makes them feel smarter and valued, so ask away. Still, some will try to wing it but be aware that discerning people of power can tell when you're lying, simply from your responses or lack thereof. Ask questions when you have to make important decisions, posing the question to strategic people to gain valuable feedback. The quickest way to engage new contacts when networking is by asking simple yet concise questions in order to gain enough information to decipher synergies between you both. This is where the power game begins and it's the most important of The Law of WALES. In the game of power, it's not what people know about you, instead, what you know about them is how you get the upper hand, so ask. Asking is the most valuable yet inexpensive method to gain information or anything else you desire in the world.

Listen

Networking is a continuous give and take, with the hopes of finding mutual passions, synergies, common interests, while at the same time exploring new territories for expansion. In addition to asking, listening is mandatory to increase your power and your net worth. For anything that helps you gather more information, has monetary value. We learn by doing, watching, asking, listening, and studying. Though we all want to share our opinions, our expertise and our experiences, knowing when to speak is just as important as knowing when to listen. When networking, make sure you listen enough to get a full grasp of what is being said, discussed or communicated. Lacking information is deadly, especially when it comes to power. Not knowing can destroy you and everything you've worked for in an instant.

Try listening to things that you have no interest in, just to learn something new. Listen to the tones of individual voices to identify changing emotions. Listen to conversations regarding the things you desire to pursue. Listen to suggestions whether you've made up your mind or not, they may present more opportunities. Listen to those who desire to share their mistakes and mishaps so that you don't repeat them. The most aware, smartest and powerful people in the world are listeners. Listen more so that you have an edge in every negotiation, circumstance, situation, even arguments.

Exchange

After watching, asking, and listening, you should be adequately equipped to effectively articulate proper responses that not only sound great but also persuade the listener or listeners. The power is now in your hands and in your mouth to contribute, to convince, to assure, to confirm, to seal or to sell. Show them you were listening by reminding them of what they shared, compliment their good points, repeating what was most important to them while adding what's important to you as well. Look for similarities, areas of agreement, how you can benefit mutually, and then share those with accuracy and enthusiasm. Finding common ground and necessity is an asset to worldwide networking and an invitation to global power. If you need clarity on anything or have more questions, ask right away so that your understanding is clear, then continue. Make sure the exchanges allow each person to get their point across. Remain ready to give feedback to show that you are paying attention.

Study

It is true to fact, knowledge is power. When presented opportunities, study to learn more about what's being presented. Study everything, old news and new information, every person and every place, let nothing go unobserved. True power is when you're able to become the researcher, the writer, the teacher, the book, and the student. To master power is to learn, teach, share, and be taught. What you know and don't know will affect your power in every aspect, with people, with your finances, with your future. I often say "Know who you're dealing with so you'll know how to deal." This means to have a greater awareness and understanding of the person you're connected to or desire to connect with, as well as who they are connected to. This is critical because most highly successful and accomplished people are busy and prioritize their time down to the minute, and none of them like wasting time.

Begin to use The Law of WALES for networking and also when you're presenting or being presented opportunities. Better yet, use them throughout life. By doing so, you will obtain an immeasurable wealth of knowledge, endless ideas and expertise from others, and commendable communication skills, which positions you to set the level of power your heart desires.

Thoughts from Bahrain

"Networking is a means to learn and impart. No man is perfect and you will always find room for improvement. When you meet other people, you get to see your own shortcomings. Positive-minded people will avail this opportunity to move toward perfection. You might also have a thing or two to teach others. And this only happens when you connect, when you network."
-Abdulaziz Khattak, Deputy Editor
Gulf Construction Magazine

Success from Mauritius

"I launched a product with some basic functionalities. But following some feedback from some of the people in my network, I was able to properly direct the product into reaching more markets. I am sure that the insights I got from them would not have been available from anyone else in the market."
-Suyash Sumaroo, Director of Codevigor Ltd

Advice from Malawi

"Good communication skills are required in order to win trust from others at a short given interaction opportunity."
-Augustine Mumba, Fund Manager, Chasefu Trading

GERMAINE MOODY

LAW 22
BE THE FIRST, NOT ANOTHER

The most powerful people in the world are often those who are the first to do something that no one else does or accomplish something that no one else has done. Networking places you in a position to connect with creators and movers & shakers from everywhere. You could easily become a part of the next big thing or become the next big thing simply by association. Power may not always come from being liked by everyone. Being different and unique is actually one of the greatest blessings to an individual. Life would be boring, dull, and downright useless if no one stood out. If you want immeasurable power, you have to change the game. This means do something different, do something better, or be the first to do it or create it. People that are in a class by themselves often have the greatest power on Earth. Not to say go and do something just for the sake of power, which you can do if you so desire, but your objective should be to tap into your own inner creativity and inspiration, attach that to those of like-mind and vision through networking, and then change the game and the world. As a society, we don't need more of the same thing, we need original and fresh thoughts, brand new inventions, and most importantly, we need the leader in you to come forth and lead the way.

Thoughts from USA
"For me in Real Estate I meet people all the time, not everyone is looking to buy or sell a house at any given moment. Most people do happen to need something at any given moment though.

Perhaps someone to do yard work, someone to work on a car, someone to fix a leaky faucet, someone to do taxes, you name it. The more contacts that I have to put two people together, the better. If I can connect person A to use person B's product or service then I make two people happy. Person B will feel they owe me as I gave them business. Person A will know I can help them and when they need someone else, or when they do decide to move, I'm the one they call. This is the beautiful reality of networking."

-Aaron Sims, Realtor

Advice from Colombia

"Show yourself as you really are, and respect the diverse points of view and interests if a relationship should be terminated. Networking is also based on values and principles. It is more than a tool or trend, it is a way of life."

-Alejandro Villada, Sales and Marketing Director

LAW 23

THE POWER OF INCLUSION

We all have the need to feel special, involved and wanted. Nobody really wants to be left all alone in life. Most people desire to be a part of something they consider valuable, meaningful, extraordinary or fun. Human beings are wired to feel better when we're included and not forgotten about. Just imagine how you would feel if your closest family member or closest friend had a special gathering of their closest family members and closest friends but you weren't invited. You'd be furious or at least disappointed. Networking connects people and it builds new relationships. Some even become as close as family members from networking. It's an amazing journey of expanding not only your network but also your life.

As a global event producer and author, I invite guests from around the world to attend my events and I invite contributors around the world to be a part of my books. Power is increased when you're able to offer your network great opportunities that include them, especially opportunities that are meaningful to them or that can expand their personal brand at the same time. Even when you refer valuable clients, customers and connections to someone in your network, this automatically raises your power level as a must-keep resource and contact in their lives. Inclusion has been used as a key to power for ages, just look at all the special clubs, member-only organizations, religious denominations, business associations, private academies and so forth. Whoever includes the most people or certain types of people, which turns into followers, automatically gain power. To capitalize on inclusion with networking, look for and create more ways to include your contacts in things that would benefit them. The more you include them, the more they'll include you.

Thoughts from Egypt

"Man is a social animal. Networking helps keep individuals socially active, for business, leisure, pleasure, fun, fact finding, research or just for while-away time. It is an essential activity to assure a person is free from feelings of neglect resulting from isolation and related depression. Building a network that is keen on what your ideals and beliefs are makes it like a family of friends and in good and bad times all are there for each other."

-Shabbir Yamani, Software Engineer

Success from Lithuania

"In order to write my latest book, I did a global research on startups surveying 1,447 startup founders and running close to 500 additional in-depth interviews. Even though I put only less than 60 real case examples in the book, more than 700 startups wanted their story to be told in my book and agreed to spend as much time as needed. I was supported by 1,447 startups all around the world, got many new friends, valuable connections and new business opportunities. I wouldn't have achieved any of this without active and sincere networking."

-Donatas Jonikas, Author "Startup Evolution Curve"

LAW 24
TRANSFER POWER

With there being multiple ways to obtain power by networking, there are also several ways to transfer it as well. Giving professional skill or performance endorsements is a sure way to share some of your power with another contact. By showing your support through an endorsement, you provide instant credibility that can add enormous value to someone's personal brand. Introductions are another easy way to transfer power. The introduction is a cousin to the endorsement and it allows you to introduce one of your connections to another, making you the first point of contact for both, which speaks volumes and can produce automatic trust between the two.

If you're a business owner, entrepreneur or promote some type of product or service, cross marketing what you do with another successful person or entity is the best public display of transferring power, which in this case, becomes a mutual transfer. Take for example Subway sandwich stores in Walmart stores or any other cross-marketing type partnership, they complement each other and everyone makes money. Now that's what I call a "power couple". Each time you connect with a new individual, your power increases. You'd be amazed just how much power you already have with your connections and how much power they can share with you. The more you communicate with them, learn about their needs, goals or pursuits, the easier it becomes to discover how, when and where to transfer your power for their benefit and of course their power for your benefit.

Thoughts from Cape Verde

"Like anything in nature we are all interdependent on each other. In order for anyone to succeed you will need the knowledge and expertise from different people so you can achieve your goals in any field in life. When networking is done right and you have access to the right people, you can easily transform the word impossible into I'm possible. This is the magic of networking."
-Saidy Andrade, Group Chairman & CEO,
Capital Consulting Group

Advice from Qatar

"Networking is the Father of Success and Mother of Development. So if you think you can do anything without the father and mother then you are on the right way to failure."
-Mehul Indravadan Sheth, Quality Control Specialist Parsons

LAW 25
DOMINATE THE EARTH

Never limit your networking. Technology allows us to text, voice chat and have visual face to face conversations with others in South Africa, Japan, Mexico, USA, France, Canada, United Kingdom, everywhere, all in the same day. We have arrived! Though your networking should always be strategic in order to achieve your goals faster, you still need to roam the world every now and then for new information and to meet exciting new people. I believe networking can teach you more than most college books if you connect with the right individuals. Reach out to the world, everyone is a SEND button away, it's absolutely mind-blowing. If you travel often or plan to travel outside of your region or country, you should always have pre-established contacts in the place of your destination. People are unprecedented and unpredictable resources, you never know when you'll need them. Don't settle for the familiar faces and those that only work in similar industries as you, expand your horizons by expanding your network. This multiplies your chances of getting your personal brand into additional circles of influence. You're then able to create opportunities and receive invites to be a part of opportunities in different parts of the world. Once you're connected, anything and everything can happen.

Having visionary global connections can change your life without a doubt. They can open up realms of abundance that you didn't even know existed. As a reminder, knowledge and communication are sure keys to power, so seek global contacts that can teach and share as much as possible with you. All of Earth is waiting to hear from you. Sharing your personal brand through networking around the world is how you dominate the Earth. You must make connections outside of your country. Take full advantage of the technology we have at our fingertips. Use the internet to learn about other ethnicities, new territories and inside information you wouldn't receive otherwise without actually visiting that region. If you desire to go a step further like I did, come up with a great idea, add in The Power of Inclusion (see Law #23) and invite your global connections to join you in on the idea. Your power will soar. It happens, I can vouch for it.

Thoughts from Guyana

"Networking holds the key for expansion and growth both personally and professionally. It unlocks the door of opportunities that are often hidden behind walls of resumes and doors of interviews."

-Carmilita Jamieson, Law Student

Success from Mexico

"In my country, developing video games is a new market, and it's difficult to find a professional developer to work with. Thanks to networking I was able to work with a great developer based in Holland, finally the project went to a successful end, and I met this great guy for my development team."

-Rodolfo Vega, CEO, Project Manager

LAW 26
CREATE MASSIVE VISIBILITY

It's now easier, faster and less expensive than ever before to become known and to be seen. Whether you have something meaningful to share or something completely inappropriate, there are billions of people around the world waiting to see it. Visibility is one of the most convincing tools to create power. People are quick to follow the celebrity-like and public figure types, good or bad, and even pay for their presence. Networking strategically at the highest levels will eventually make you visible, this comes natural. If you desire astronomic power, you can use your network to create massive visibility for you, not just in exclusive circles of influence and affluence but also front and center in the world's view.

Film, TV, Radio, Print & Online Media

By now you should have a profile on Linkedin or the latest leading social network for professionals. If not, stop reading right here and go set one up then return. It's time to focus on making connections in the following industries to enhance your visibility: Broadcast Media, Online Media, Publishing, Media Production, Motion Pictures, Marketing & Advertising, Entertainment, Writing & Editing, Public Relations, etc. The people that can place you in a film (motion picture, short, documentary), on television (talk show, news, tv commercial, cable, internet, mobile), feature you in a magazine or newspaper (print, online), have you as a guest on their radio show (satellite, online) or give you any other type of media attention will be found in these industries. If they can't do it themselves, the majority of them know someone who can. These contacts are mighty assets to power and extremely valuable to your network. I recommend seeking out ones in larger cities, though local is the best place to start for most to create content for your media portfolio. All you have to do is compose a short, kind and detailed personal message to all of them explaining who you are and request assistance, suggestions or referrals they can offer to help you obtain media attention. That's all it takes to get the ball rolling. You'll be surprised at how many people will respond to advise you. Get over the fear of rejection, you're on these professional sites to network. Ignore and get rid of anyone that responds hostile and negatively towards you, some will, but thank those that respond positively, especially those with referrals or great advice, and always offer to assist them in any way you can as well.

Secure as many interviews, features, appearances and engagements that you can from your contacts and their referrals. You could be asked to co-host a show, sit on a panel for a conference, partner on a future project, write a column, become a guest blogger or spokesperson. Believe me, anything can happen when you just reach out to people. I know because I've experienced it all. There are no limitations when you network. If a magazine is really interested in what you have going on, ask for the cover. Covers are always more powerful than just another feature on the inside of a publication. Don't be rude or ungrateful but be strategic and show them how what you bring to the table can also enhance their media brand. Be sure to share all of this media attention with your social media networks. This will create intrigue, followers, connections, more opportunities and more visibility. Create long-term relationships with your media connections. It only takes one of them for a stratospheric jump on the power meter.

Press Releases

A press release is an official statement issued to media outlets that gives them information on a particular matter. You should take advantage of the free press release websites to release information about yourself, your company, brand, organization or whatever information you want to get out. There are thousands you can search and use, plus most of the releases can be accessed through search engines at any time for reference. There are also more premium services that send your releases to more branded news and media outlets. You can write it yourself or find someone more experienced. Just stick to the basics but make it sound like a big deal, something worth reading, with an intriguing headline, and always share the Who, What, When, Why, and Where. Most media outlets require that you send them a press release or bio, so go ahead and have that ready before you even reach out to your media connections for help.

Videos & Vlogs

The most popular way to increase your visibility on a local, national or global scale with little to no money is through video. You can discuss certain topics, demonstrate products and services, teach a class, dance, eat or just stare into the camera and become an online sensation for no reason at all. As for visibility for your personal brand, videos and vlogs are an inexpensive and a great way to market yourself to your network, while allowing them to market you to their network, and also set yourself up on the global stage. Share the videos with your professional network and all of your social media. Videos online can garner massive visibility, boosting your power literally in minutes. They can also position you for new streams of income, including speaking engagements, appearances, sponsorships, partnerships, film & tv deals, in addition to generating media interviews and features.

Sample Email To Media Contacts

Here's a sample message that you can use when reaching out to your media contacts for visibility assistance:

Greetings Sarah,

I wanted to let you know that I'm truly grateful for the opportunity to be a part of your network, I consider it a privilege and honor. I'd also like to share that I'm an author and motivational speaker, and would love to be introduced or referred to any of your media connections that you think would be beneficial to helping me increase visibility for what I do. Any appearances, interviews, features, or press would be more than appreciated. Also, if I can assist you in any way to contribute to your continued success in life, please let me know and I'm all in. Thank you for your time friend. Have an incredible day!

Thoughts from Singapore

"The global "squeeze" of the world with technology has rendered all of us neighbors with one another. This means that we are able to reach out to a lot more people easily, but it also means that you have the power to shape opinions and perceptions. To this extent, online networking is so important, since it helps others to find you. Be it through a blog post on Forbes, Entrepreneur, or Huffington Post article (where I regularly contribute at), online networking brings the eyeballs to you the right way, if you know how. That can mean extremely lucrative opportunities for your career and life. The second aspect is physical networking, meaning face to face networking events. In my first entrepreneurship chapter as a networking events startup, we used to emphasise on the importance of networking to participants, and how, if they mastered the skill, they would enhance their relationships and net worth. And you know what? They did. In summary, it's not what you know, or who you know. It's about who knows you, and it's about how well you craft that perception for yourself."

-John Chen, Head Writer, Digital Marketing Consultant

Advice from Slovakia

"Don't wait until the world will find you. Be proactive, search for new contacts and when you have something to say, say it, don't wait for a better moment, because the best moment is right at the second when you have the desire and passion to do it. Also market yourself every single time you have the opportunity."

-Martina Kičinová, CRM & Digital Marketing Specialist

GERMAINE MOODY

People.

People are your greatest asset when it comes to networking.

Without them, you will not exist. People will be involved in your angelic climb or your demon-infested fall. The kind of people you surround yourself with is what matters. This, you should take heed to immediately. Some people are for your good while others are sheep in wolves clothing, angels of darkness, awaiting the next opportunity to try and sabotage everything you've worked for. Don't be fooled, they could be in your family, a best friend, or even the one sleeping next to you. Some are strategically sent to stop you but you shall prevail with the proper knowledge. Everyone must be evaluated constantly. They should be tested through your highs and lows, through your pain or your power. Only those that can stand and fight for you should remain, let everyone else go quickly. Guard your circle. You will not need everyone. You only need those that were born to be a part of your journey, those that are sent to encourage you, teach you, protect you, pray for you, guide you, correct you, expand your vision and open doors. Let this guide your networking.

LAW 27

FOOLS WITH THEIR OPINIONS & NEGATIVITY

Anyone with the audacity to openly and publicly bring negative energy into an atmosphere of opportunity will also stab you in the back at the first opportunity as well.

All networkers are not created equal and not everyone you connect with will be as excited and as optimistic as you are. Matter of fact, some are the exact opposite, unfortunately. The truth of the matter is, we all operate on different levels, some on lower frequencies than others, and these lower frequency types tend to have an opinion about everything, mostly negative, so these you should kindly avoid. Ever been in a situation when someone mentions a topic, an idea, an opportunity, in the form of a post on a social network, and all the responses are great and optimistic until one person says something to completely dismantle the life out of hope itself? And the weird thing is, their comment doesn't even make sense. There are those out there in the networking world who believe they know everything and also believe that it's their divine assignment to change what you think you know. Beware of these people, they are like diseases that seek out a physical body to attack. Don't trust them. Anyone with the audacity to openly and publicly bring negative energy into an atmosphere of opportunity will also stab you in the back at the first opportunity as well.

There is so much negativity in the world, in our communities, on our televisions, on our computers, even on our phones. People network to expand their lives, to learn, to grow, to add value and fulfillment, not to debate everything or listen to naysayers and doubters constantly. Mind you, opinions can be great assets, they open you up to think and expand as well, but only allow opinions that come from a good place to be entertained. The foolish types have no better joy than adding lonely and negative toddlers to their crib of depression. Pay them no mind and don't respond, let them cry and cry until they fall asleep.

Thoughts from Germany

"Business, Politics, Arts - it's all about humanity and the connections we make. As the world's population starts hiding behind their smartphones and laptops - it's more important than ever to network with each other. We all play many roles - parents, siblings, coworkers, boyfriends, mentors, neighbors - within each of these roles we have an obligation to communicate. To share. To help each other in times of need or to fulfill the human potential. Networking and building networks makes life whole."

-William Toll, VP Marketing

Success from Yemen

"Networking paved the way for me to overcome the difficulties and to see all difficulties as possible. I understand now that it is not impossible to realize dreams no matter how much opposition you face. I have arrived to what I dreamed and more. I am now in a high level position in my country and the world, and networking helped me get to here."

-Abdulaziz Bahaj, Head of Yemeni National Security

GERMAINE MOODY

LAW 28
DISREGARD TIME WASTERS

These types of people can be tricky. As for networking, they'll start off just fine, friendly conversations, which is great, but then after weeks, months or years, the networking never amounted to anything nor did you learn anything new. Now don't get me wrong, it's fine to create new friends along the way and you will, but in order to waste less time and to accomplish more of your goals, make sure you prioritize how many connections you have time to reply to about absolutely nothing. It can and will get overwhelming and frustrating when you find yourself communicating with so many people but not making any progress with your life, to-do list, career or goals. Time wasters indeed exist in the networking world and they need people like you to keep them busy. Don't fall for it.

Time wasters will talk to you about anything, their family, their past travels, what they wish they could do, how much they dislike their job, and so on. Hopefully you won't come across too many of them that complain about what they want to do (though they aren't pursuing it) or about what others are doing, these are the worst kind. It bothers me to be around or even associated with people who always have something to complain about. It's a waste of oxygen. I instantly stop responding to them and return to a life of possibilities. You must do the same. And for those time-wasting networkers you come across who get bored often, get rid of them immediately. There's too many people to connect to, too much money to be made for yourself and to help create a better world, and entirely too much to do for anyone to be bored in this lifetime.

Thoughts from South Africa

"Networking is an essential tool in any person's business or private life. There are circumstances that could have turned out much differently if only the correct people were involved at the time."

-Byron Nel, Project Manager

Advice from Luxembourg

"Never forget to smile! Be polite! Don't forget to use friendly approach but still be diplomatic at least at the beginning. Listen to the others, do not interrupt. Always exchange contact details! Sometimes your enemies might have key roles in your professional or business development, so respect them and analyze them carefully!"

-Joanna Koleva, Marketing Consultant

DON'T WASTE TIME IMPRESSING THE WRONG PEOPLE

A master networker is like a magician to time. The greater you become at networking, the faster success and advancement will appear, while your audience remains in awe of how you made years of expected work and challenges completely disappear.

There's nothing wrong with connecting with a variety of people, I actually recommend it, but when it comes to taking care of business and making swift progress, your networking must be targeted. All research, every referral, every word, every person, every email, every event, every social network post, every call and every meeting must be calculated and aimed to achieve your goal. I've known countless individuals that network on a whim, year after year, making no real progress on gathering resourceful connections, leaving them hopeless and ready to give up. They have no plan, no strategy, no insight, no direction, no market research, and they end up wasting time impressing the wrong people. It's one thing to waste time on your own, that's bad enough. It's even worse to waste time trying to impress the wrong people because now you're wasting their time as well. Most are unaware of the time they waste and this why a great majority never accomplish much. Old classmates, ex-lovers, co-workers, friends and even family members may not be of much use to advance your career or life purpose yet still, many tire themselves attempting to prove something to people who aren't qualified to advance them. Some people burn out right before success arrives because of this.

If you desire to achieve influence, wealth and power faster than most, then you need to be connected to those who can help you get there a lot quicker. There is a circle of influential, wealthy, powerful and successful people in the world. Most are all interconnected in some way through one or two degrees of separation. You can take a lifetime to build from the ground up or you can allow networking to provide a shortcut to the decision makers, gatekeepers and power circles. Don't waste any more time impressing the wrong people, instead, use networking to skip the line and go straight to the top, positioning you with resourceful connections that you can benefit from and vice versa. A master networker is like a magician to time. The greater you become at networking, the faster success and advancement will appear, while your audience remains in awe of how you made years of expected work and challenges completely disappear.

Thoughts from Belgium

"Synergy makes the whole of us greater than the sum of our parts. This also applies for networking and by creating synergy using your networking, you create opportunity."
-*Sofiane Chami, Entrepreneur*

Success from Jordan

"Thanks to networking I was able to reach the position of an Executive Director at the age of 26. I managed to reach that point through building a large network of people who are working in my field, a network of partners, supporters, and clients. This caused my Board of Directors to decide to promote me twice in the same year and hire me as an Executive Director."
-*Mohammad Obaidat, Shamal Start Incubator Manager*

LAW 30
REMOVE SMALL THINKERS

A lot of people have been conditioned, raised and educated to have a status quo mindset. Their vision doesn't extend any further than their right or left arm. You will come across these types as well in your networking. Some may even tell you that what you are pursuing is impossible. Small thinkers get intimidated easily and that intimidation turns into jealousy or admiration over time. Those who are quick to combat your biggest ideas, lofty thoughts and optimism, will also easily turn against you. Not all small thinkers are bad for you though. A select few may cause you to reevaluate your success strategy and to go even bigger. For the rest of them, the ones who manufacture constant doubt, frustration and animosity should be dismissed, removed and ignored immediately. Keep in mind that though networking surrounds you with people who are eager to connect and explore synergies, not everyone you meet will be comfortable in the atmosphere of possibilities that now you operate in.

Thoughts from South Korea

"Networking is very important to me as an entrepreneur. It is like a piece that can complete the puzzle, like an encyclopedia or google that can answer your questions, like an uber that you can call anytime, anywhere and can bring you anywhere you want."
-Cristy Kim, CEO
Lord and Goldman International Consulting Inc.

Advice from Kenya

"Never think an opportunity to network is a waste of time. It may not give success right away, but you never know whom you are talking to and their connections, so keep an open mind."

-Julie Balcombe, Management Consultant

LAW 31

BEWARE OF DEMONS IN DISGUISE

Success breeds resentment in those that are unhappy with their own lives, especially if you're successful at something that they've tried to do or never had the boldness to do.

Just as sure as you meet networkers to help you be more successful, you will unfortunately at times, hopefully not too many times, come across those that secretly want to see you fail. It's always good to test the waters of those that want to connect with you. By careful observation, evaluation, plus patience, you'll eventually be made aware of their intentions and purpose. I've come across a handful of people who for some reason or another did not like me. To this day I still don't know why. They've never told me why, never questioned me about why and they've never met me, yet they've tried to do malicious things to try and destroy my name and my character but to no avail. I consider these demons in disguise, and by demons I mean real demons. Anyone who tries to destroy the present and future plans that God has preset for you is being led by an opposing spirit, a demon. These unhappy and unfulfilled individuals obviously have too much free time on their hands. My mentors told me that this comes with success and that all successful people should be prepared for it. You better believe they are out there and your level of awareness will assist you with identifying them faster. Success breeds resentment in those that are unhappy with their own lives, especially if you're successful at something that they've tried to do or never had the boldness to do.

It's not your responsibility to babysit these types but it is your responsibility to warn others who ask you about them. When one of your current connections has a history of backstabbing people, lying on people, unsuccessful friendships, making negative comments publicly on social media and the other, you should take heed. I had to learn this the hard way because I sincerely believe in giving everyone the benefit of the doubt. I will say, that through my worldwide networking, for the most part, people are naturally good people, but there's always an undercover bad apple here and there. If you don't have an inner peace about one of your connections, you should reach out to them and get to know them. This opens up the window to find out if your assumptions were right or wrong. Evaluate your connections when your instinct alerts you to do so. Keep good hearted, hard-working, smart-working and loving individuals around you. Those are the best connections to have. They will be there to support you in your professional life and some will even be there as a good friend when you need one.

Thoughts from Hungary
"Networking is a way for recognizing and understanding different minds, approaches, thoughts. We are always on the road to be mentors and mentees at the same time."
-Gabor Pinter, Founder of Mind Mate Inspiration

Thoughts from Bulgaria
"I love technology and finding ways of using technology to create sustainable businesses. I visit a lot of entrepreneurial events around town and meet all sorts of people through networking. One time I met a science/space guy. We talked about what motivates us and one thing led to another, so that in several months I was traveling to NASA to study exponential technologies and entrepreneurship."
-Sergey Petrov, CTO at Bee Smart Technologies

LAW 32
BUILD WITH LEADERS & MOTIVATORS

Motivation is the great stabilizer that keeps people sane.

My favorite people in the world are the leaders and motivators. The more of these types you network with, the more exciting, optimistic and fulfilled your networking and life will be. Seek them out, search for them, encourage them and support them because they will do the same for you. It's obvious that there is a lack of leadership in the world today. Networking is not just to get ahead, networking is also to encourage one another, to connect with other humans and push mankind forward. We are all connected in more ways than we know, we have more in common than we do differences, and we all need motivation and someone to show us the way. This is why networking with people that are leaders and motivators is so important. Many of you reading this right now are in that same category. Matter of fact, it should be the desire of everyone reading this to become a leader and motivator as a networker. This is what fuels real networking. You don't have to make a big speech to be a leader and you don't need a television or academic platform to motivate people. All you need is the joy of seeing and helping people all succeed.

Leaders
Whenever there is a significant movement, shift, advancement or new way of thinking for the human race, it is preceded by a leader. Whenever there is a major invention that revolutionizes the world

as we know it, it is created by a leader. Leaders keep us moving forward. Without them, there would be little to no progress. They come in all shapes, sizes, backgrounds, and they have their own way of doing things. True leaders are almost always optimistic and overflowing with hope. You can tell the great ones by how they respond to challenging circumstances and unfortunate events. Even through back and forth conversations when you message them, you'll be able to sense there's something different and unique. Maintaining a certain level of hope and assurance is a shared characteristic by several leaders. They often evangelize the best is yet to come in every situation. Be wise to connect with and stay connected to as many great leaders as you can when networking. These are the people you want around you, on your team and in your life forever because they are magnets for opportunity and success. They attract great people by the droves and can expand your network of contacts instantly, most times beyond comprehension. Seek out the leaders, befriend them and prepare to be the leader you were born to be as well.

Motivators

Even though there are those who believe the world is a depressing place, the world would be even more depressing if it wasn't for the daily motivators that we come across in-person, online, television, radio, etc. Motivation is the great stabilizer that keeps people sane. Networkers love motivation and it takes motivation in order to network. Everyone needs motivation whether they will admit it or not. On the other hand, if you don't like motivation or motivational people then I suggest you cease all of your networking. You won't get that far being a plane Jane, with lifeless greetings, posts and messages. I've discovered that the most successful networkers and the most successful people all have a passion to motivate, it's like a fire in a sense. Fire is attractive and it spreads fast, which is why motivators are so valuable around the world. They transfer fire and expectancy.

Networking is exciting, it's empowering and it's invigorating. If you really want to see your networking explode and doors swing wide open, do what the motivators do, motivate the contacts you have and the future contacts you meet. Encourage what they're working on and always say things like "That is awesome, I'm so excited for you". Motivators also tend to have a more optimistic outlook and a more positive perception than most people. Becoming a motivator is one of the skills to dominating the game of networking. It's not only attractive to the majority, it's also enticing to power players, decision makers and the world's wealthiest individuals. I'm a serial motivator, and since becoming one, access to the world and everything within it has opened up to me, every limitation has been destroyed. You should work on becoming one as well to take your life and your networking to greater heights.

Thoughts from Chile

"Networking is one of the most powerful tools an entrepreneur or a businessman can use to grow their company. Networking opens up new opportunities and creates synergies between parts that normally wouldn't meet."
-Leonardo Nunes Ricucci,
CEO and Co-founder of Novalact Life Sciences

Advice from Venezuela

"We need each other, you can't be alone in any endeavor you plan. Give and help to others, seize every opportunity you have to know new people and become more connected every day."
-Felix Bolivar, Co-Founder, Business Developer

LAW 33
LEVERAGE EVERYONE

Trust me, it takes more than talent and education to make it to the top. A networker knows this, so they leverage everyone to get to where they want to be, so should you.

People are your most valuable asset in networking. Over the years, the degrees of separation have dramatically decreased. We are now more connected than ever. This presents you with a phenomenal amount of leverage, so use everyone in your network and those in their network to your advantage. If you don't have a certain type of connection, reach out to someone in your network that does. This goes for any situation, circumstance or opportunity where you need a specific type of individual or strategic person by name. In many business dealings, people are quick to drop names to show affiliation or association as a way to build credibility, you should do the same when necessary or expected. Don't be afraid to disclose a powerful name that's in your network or circle. Influential, affluent and ultra-successful people feel more comfortable when they know you're affiliated with someone they know as well. Your associations alone through networking can take your clout and bargaining power to new levels automatically.

Everyone Is Valuable But Networkers Are A-List

I believe everyone you connect with has some value but let's cut to the chase, the most powerful networkers are the A-list ones who can put you in front of the right people, in the right situations or give you the right information to propel you. These are tremendously connected people, several with global networks. Once you get on their good side, it only takes one email, text or call from them on your behalf to help catapult you to the next level. It's happened to me several times on my climb, and now I do it for others as well. Be sure you invite them to be a part of your opportunities and always support their pursuits and projects, for this is a way to get into global circles of networkers, which is where you need to be. Little do people know, some of Hollywood's biggest stars are where they are today because they've mastered networking. Same goes for several politicians and world leaders. Trust me, it takes more than talent and education to make it to the top. A networker knows this, so they leverage everyone to get to where they want to be, so should you.

Thoughts from Bahamas

"It is not complex: understanding and knowing the "right people" will allow you to get to places that you could not achieve otherwise. While there are many benefits of networking, the most important may be obtaining a new job or even acquiring a new business, and having associations with key individuals who can assist you in the future. Networking can open up new doorways for you personally and professionally. In regards to job hunting, and in a marketplace that is incredibly aggressive, networking could be the difference between getting the job or that contract or not. Finally, it is about the associations: the types that are possible to construct through networking are priceless."

-Jerome G. Sherman, President JSLocal Seo Service

Success from Burkina Faso

"Thanks to networking, my books are now best-sellers. My company departments are now supported and I'm making amazing friends around the world."

-Harouna Timothée KABORE, Entrepreneur

GERMAINE MOODY

LAW 34
CAREFULLY SELECT YOUR TEAM

*Most people accomplish very little in life because they never
reached out to the right people for help.*

Now that you're aware of Fools With Their Opinions &
Negativity, Time Wasters, Impressing The Wrong People, Small
Thinkers, Demons In Disguise and Leaders & Motivators, you are
prepared to create a mental picture of the people you need to
network with and those that you don't. Once your goals are set,
there are key connections to keep around for the journey, be it for
advice, long-term encouragement, mentorship and of course
assistance in achieving those goals. I call these individuals your
"Destiny Team". Your "Destiny Team" are the people divinely
sent to help you accomplish your dreams and complete your
mission in life, thus fulfilling your destinations. They come in all
sizes, shapes, colors, ages, and from all backgrounds, regions,
countries and religions. They are the most important people you
will ever meet, that is, if you're smart enough to get on the path.
Several arrive periodically throughout life but the bulk of the
powerhouses show up once you accept what you were put on Earth
to do and begin to network strategically toward it.

Define Who Belongs On Your Destiny Team

First, you need to know what type of people should be on your Destiny Team. Connecting with those who are already doing what you desire to do is a great place to start and it only takes one person to get the ball rolling. The greater your communication skills, the more professional you'll appear so that you're taken seriously, the better you'll be understood and the more access you'll get to highly successful people. Regardless of who you contact first, compliment them on any present or past achievements and remember to thank them for their valuable time in your initial message. When they realize that you understand the value of time, they'll give you more of theirs. Make it a point to ask detailed questions that require a resourceful or strategic answer, don't waste time with useless jargon, get to the point. You can ask them for a referral, a recommendation or any direction to help you move toward your goals. Do this connection by connection, and you'll soon have several new potentials to review for your Destiny Team, and you're already making headway on the path of your dreams.

Recruit Your Destiny Team

You'll come across all kinds of people as you network. The key to deciding who to keep around will depend on your own personality and ability to deal with others. Some may be passive, others aggressive. It's best that you focus more on who can help you, period. Whether you like their clothes, their outlook on life, their religion, their ethnic background or whatever, you need to stay focused on the big picture and not minor things. I've worked with a few people in the past that disagreed with me on several things but we both agreed that we could make positive change in the world as well as more money by working together and not separate. I challenge you to leap out of your comfort zone when networking and recruiting your Destiny Team. You should purposely look for those that challenge and stretch you to think higher and become greater, even to the point where it upsets you at times, but not all the time. After getting recommendations and referrals, do your research to see who appeals to your professional outlook the most. If you have to join organizations, become a member of online groups, make a cameo at an event, or whatever it calls for, do what must be done to find the people you need on your team. Most people accomplish very little in life because they never reached out to the right people for help. You can also use the "mentor" card to get a successful person on your team. People love sharing what they know, it gives them a sense of importance and value, so don't be afraid to ask someone if they'll be your mentor. Let them know that all you request is any advice they are willing to share, a referral or two if needed and an occasional check-in here and there. Never place a lot of pressure on someone you request to mentor you. Keep it lite and simple.

Deploy Your Destiny Team

Now that you have the first leg of your Destiny Team, more will arrive as your journey of life continues, but for now this current team must be positioned on the battlefield for influence, wealth and power. You can begin reaching out to them, requesting advice or any assistance they can offer, as well as offering to assist them in any way that you can. As you continue conversations, show interest in what's next on their agenda. If they have events coming up near you or where you have access to, offer to volunteer to help out. Your goal is to build trust and a great friendship, which is accomplished by communication, encouragement and supporting one another. This will cause your Destiny Team to do more for you than you ask, like promote you, recommend books, include you in on special event invitations, etc. Stay progressive at all times because nothing attracts successful people more than other progressive and successful people. People consider it a privilege to be a part of someone else's success. Keep that in mind and your Destiny Team will automatically bring more team members in to help you achieve anything, even take over the world if that's your goal.

Thoughts from New Zealand

"I have learned that you can only go so far on your own. To make a real difference or to turn an idea into a tangible reality you must build a team, or group of people who share your goals and vision. Finding these people is only possible, I believe, through effective networking."

-Chris Hanlon, Educator and Filmmaker

Advice from Sri Lanka

"Remember without networking, you are like nothing even though you are educated. No networking means you will be isolated in the world and this can cause you to become poor in all terms."

-Chamara Bandara, CEO SCB Corporate

LAW 35

OBSERVATION PRECEDES STRATEGY

There's a difference between looking at something and observing it. The majority go through life watching yet never observing, never paying attention to the opportune seasons of change, never giving careful thought to what makes things go right and what makes them go wrong, never properly analyzing and evaluating themselves year after year. This results in billions of people who are uncertain of who they are and unaware of what they should be doing with their lives. I've discovered that most of life's questions can be answered by a life dedicated to observation. Learning to utilize networking to gain influence, wealth and power falls under the same rule. Observation is the cheapest form of market research and the most inexpensive way to obtain knowledge. A review of past conversations or encounters between you and your contacts should provide a wealth of knowledge to enhance future communication with past, present and future connections. Observe how they communicate, how they responded and the things they responded to.

The more you observe, the greater the strategy you can create to master each connection and build allies all over the world. Take into account everything you learn from the people you meet, and use that information to make greater decisions with new connections. This is exactly what I do to determine the networking climate and temperature of my connections. It gives you the upper hand. It shows them that you're attentive and have taken time to learn more without having to question them about everything. It's the greatest feeling for me when someone mentions or congratulates me on one of my ventures, books, accomplishments, or projects without me mentioning it first. Master observation for networking and for every area of life. You'll gain the knowledge needed to develop a winning strategy that compels your connections to become powerful soldiers on behalf.

Thoughts from Canada

"Networking and making connections is very important for there is power to effect positive change when you have large numbers of aligned participants. The more that we connect and share, the more that we can succeed in any endeavour or goal that we have."
-Laurie K. Grant, CEO & Founder, FutureWave Group Inc

Success from Aruba

"Networking helped me become elected Minister of Health and Sports for Aruba, where I was able to move the island from one heavy island to one healthy island from 2009 – 2013."
-Richard Visser, CEO and Co-Founder
Vera Health and Education

LAW 36
PREPARATION PRECEDES MASTERY

There is no substitute for preparation. To become a master networker, you need to study the best of the best and make sure your communication skills are up to par. Study interviews of successful people, watch videos, read articles, and if you can listen in on conference calls or observe serial networkers at networking events, take full advantage of it all. You will only become great through preparation, and that goes for everything in life. With networking, you will become greater faster by studying those that have mastered it. Practice meeting different people when you're out and about, always smile and remain friendly, even though some people will consider that odd these days, do it anyway. Ask super networkers in your network how they prefer to be greeted or approached when connecting. Get as much insight on finding what most professionals prefer and then use this information to help you compose the right communication rhythm and approach that is still authentically you. It must become as natural as breathing. Your constant observation and preparation positions you to flow in a variety of situations with a wide range of individuals.

Thoughts from Western Sahara
"Networking allows a global range to our thinking, to our action and to the impact we want to have. It removes the barriers of geography, timing and boundaries. It also gives us the ability to choose and target, and to aim well at whom we want to be in touch with. Over the years it has become a powerful weapon in the hands of change agents, creators and seekers."
-*Mohamed Yeslem Beisat, Former Diplomat and Governor*

Advice from Belize

"Always make sure your information paints a true picture of you and of what you do. Once the connection is made, continue to work on reinforcing it while keeping your goals in the forefront. Networking is one of the most inexpensive ways to meet a wide range of people in the whole world, it also allows you to narrow down to persons with your interest and similar professional status. Networking is a must to be able to get known and to know what others are doing."

-Joy Godfrey, Managing Director

LAW 37
AFFILIATION PRECEDES POWER

No matter what you think or what people say, who you know does matter. Matter of fact, who you know can open up doors much faster when networking than anything else. One introduction alone can shift your entire existence. In certain circles, you can't even enter without some sort of recommendation or referral. This is the power of affiliation and you must leverage it constantly. Those in your network can provide advancement to your own success just by acknowledging the connection. I've seen it happen thousands of times in my conversations and business deals. When people know that you're connected to others they respect or others of esteem, prominence, stature, influence, power or wealth, that automatically increases your clout. It's safe yet unfortunate to say that who you know can actually make you a powerhouse even before you accomplish anything on your own. Why, because you then become a valuable gatekeeper to those who desire to connect with your affiliations.

This goes beyond just people though. Organizations, associations, clubs, teams, schools, and more are affiliations that can be just as important to increase your power in the game of networking and accomplishing your goals. People associate your level of intellect, expertise, professionalism and power by your affiliations. Every new connection comes with new affiliations. It's wise to check out your connection's affiliations because most people are so busy networking until they fail to realize just how powerful their circles are already. There's nothing wrong with dropping a name here and there. If you're a gatekeeper or serial networker, trust me, someone has dropped your name as well for credibility, to break the ice or to advance in some way. It happens to me all the time and I found that it only increases your power. Sometimes your name alone won't open the door but instead the name of someone you know or something you're connected to will. If you have the affiliation, by all means use it. Everyone and everything needs to provide some type of value for you to increase your power.

Thoughts from Italy

"Networking has now been empowered by the internet and the web. Today most of the online activities are made without a physical interaction. We are in the networking generation where not only business opportunities are possible but so is everything else. Social Media gives you the chance to connect with who you want, anywhere in the world. This is the real revolution."
-*Stefano Mongardi, Entrepreneur*

Success from Brazil

"My business came to life because of my network, and in turn my network has helped it grow and expand. I'm a connector, I bring the right people together for their business and that has led to startups getting funded and companies fostering innovation with new partnerships from these connections."
-*Pamela Granoff, Founder, Latam Founders Network*

Purpose.

Why were you born? What are you here for? Networking gives you a lot of options to meet endless amounts of people and create multitudes of new experiences but what is it worth if your soul is unfulfilled? Networking is so mighty until it not only places you in a position to live a more purpose-driven life, it also gives you great power to provide resources for others to live one as well. It is amazing what a life can accomplish when it discovers the purpose for its creation.

LAW 38

BE A CONDUIT FOR OTHERS

You carry great power as a networker, more than you know. One of the main keys to getting everything you want in life is to be connected to the people that can help make it happen. This means that networking is essential, even though most humans ever actually acknowledge it or even realize it. Not enough attention has been given to the art of networking, the necessity of it, and the danger of living without it. You may have been searching for gatekeepers in the past but as you network more and more, you will become a gatekeeper as well. People will soon contact you for help and assistance just as you did in the beginning. When they do reach out to you, be nice, friendly and provide as much help as possible. Whether it's referrals, connections, resources, sound advice that someone else taught you, or disclosing some of the things you've mastered or had to overcome, share it. Find purpose in helping someone else become a success, that's what networking is all about. People may not remember everything you said but they'll remember what you did for them. Never think that it's just about you. Everyone is on a separate journey, and the path isn't always as bright for others. So give, give, give, as much advice as you can and help, help, help. Make being a conduit for others to succeed a mandatory part of your networking. If you do, I promise you that whoever you need to know and whatever you need on your journey will show up automatically.

Thoughts from Pakistan

"We humans have an innate desire to feel connected, to share stories of triumph and tribulations, to be understood and loved, and to be there for each other when the going gets tough. Networking helps us quench this thirst for connection, relationships, communication and understanding. In the business world, networking is more important and (for most people) much harder at the same time."

-Syed Irfan Ajmal, CEO MQC, Forbes Columnist

Advice from Guam

"You must dare to be open minded, free, diverse and accepting that someone will have a better idea than you or someone will compliment your idea by providing a solution you had not thought of. Dare to be different, dare to be diverse and dare to live your dream. To be successful is to open your world and network, network, network."

-Vera Topasna, Executive Vice President

LAW 39
MAKE A DIFFERENCE

I haven't met anyone on the planet that has found complete fulfillment in just becoming wealthy. Whether we are aware of it or not, all humans are spiritually connected to one another and also share the pain of someone else. This makes it almost impossible to gain great success and not share some of it with those who need help. Though you've worked extremely hard for it, networked day in and day out, and sacrificed tremendously, your success and wealth must also benefit others at some point. I'm not saying give all your money away, but you can start supporting education programs in your community or build a community center, give to youth organizations, donate annually to food missions that feed the less fortunate, support a charity that assists veterans, give advice to a group that needs guidance, or start your own nonprofit foundation to support charitable efforts of your choice. Do something other than hoard your success, influence, wealth and power for your own gain. It will only rot and run out if you do. As long as you are granted success, it is a divine mandate to give back. This is something most of the rich and successful live by already, so go ahead and make it a part of your life mission and networking strategy now. Somebody really needs you to be successful. Your life was meant to help them do the same, that's just how serious your existence is. You are needed more than know. Never forget that.

All of your giving doesn't have to be financial. Just by networking and meeting people from all over the world, you'll amass great knowledge and experience that could be shared in a variety of ways to inspire others. Becoming a mentor is the perfect way to teach someone else the ropes and hold them accountable for staying on target with their goals. Sharing the importance of networking is also something you should readily advocate because it applies to everyone. Networking is educational on so many levels. The things you learn along the way from people, including the opportunities you receive can pay off way more than any certificate or degree ever could. Combine the two and you'll be set for an unlimited life.

Heal The World

Networking allows you to help yourself and others directly, it also enables you to be a part of even greater works and opportunities that could change the world. When I decided to take my networking globally by getting to know more professional connections in Australia, China, South America, Canada, Japan, France, Sweden, South Africa and more, my entire life changed for the better. I entered a new circle of knowledge and possibilities. It has also occurred to me that people genuinely want to be connected to one another. I've had conversations with someone from just about every part of the world, even translating conversations into English for my understanding. I also discovered that billions of people around the world need help, especially organizations that assist the less fortunate, the sick, the wounded, the discouraged. Your network gives you influence and access to shed light and awareness where it's needed, enabling you to use your network for a higher purpose.

Whether it's sharing a non-profit website address with your connections, becoming a spokesperson for a charity, joining an advisory board, recruiting volunteers from your country for a global cause or something else, networking allows you to be a part of or initiate great change. This shouldn't be taken lightly. By building your connections worldwide, you can help perform what some people will consider miracles. Many a times, I've used networking to bring immediate awareness to causes, in addition to producing global projects and raising money to benefit unfortunate circumstances worldwide that are close to my heart. Becoming a master networker can grant you access to do whatever you desire in your lifetime. Influence, wealth and power will meet you face to face if you follow the path of the laws in this book. On your journey, keep in mind that when you are divinely given access to influence, wealth, and power, there is a greater purpose for it than just influence, wealth and power. That purpose, is to help make the world a better place, for all of us.

Thoughts from Democratic Republic Of The Congo
"Through networking we can learn from each other. We can share ideas that can change the world and important information that can also save someone's life."
-Noella Kisembo, Founder of Expression Artistique de la Jeunesse

Success from Seychelles
"Networking has enabled me to save rare birds threatened by extinction by harnessing expertise and funding from 30 different organisations in my country and 20 others from all over the world."
-Nirmal Shah, CEO Nature Seychelles

Advice from Palestine
"Network, network, network, for your own personal goals and for that of others, who need your voice, your potential to make their lives better, for making this world a better place for all."
-Fatima Butmah, Independent Consultant

GERMAINE MOODY

Legacy.
Your journey on Earth should be so powerful that when you transition to the next realm, it'll be like you never left. The lives you touched, the hopeless you inspired, the less fortunate you helped, the opportunities and assistance you were able to provide for so many because you became the ultimate you, this is true legacy. The things you were born to do are directly tied to the people you were destined to connect with in order to make it all happen. You must use networking to find those people already waiting in position to help develop you into your ultimate self, or your legacy will be incomplete.

LAW 40

DO WHAT MOST PEOPLE WON'T DO

People that stand out are normally the ones that get the most attention and opportunities in life. Being average and normal won't help you reach your ultimate influence, wealth or power. From my experience and business relationships with some of the richest, intriguing and most innovative minds, I've concluded that when you do what most people won't do, you can have what most people will never have. This book isn't for those who want to just get by or just be happy. This book is for those who want it all, to be happy, influential, wealthy and powerful. It takes boldness to stand out. It takes even more boldness to reach out to people you don't know, to network and put yourself in a position to be rejected or ignored. Networking is not about who doesn't respond to you or those you don't connect with. It's about the connections that you do make, those that support you, collaborate with you, and build with you. A lot of people want success but they don't want to work or endure sacrifices and embarrassment for it. They want influence but don't want to build their network and connections around the world. They want wealth but don't want to learn about creating value, investing or developing multiple streams of income. They want power but lack commitment to the grind it takes to create a brand or name for themselves. To achieve what most people will never achieve, you have to do what most people will never do.

The influence, wealth and power gap is completely obvious to everyone on the planet. Only a handful of people run the world. You must use networking to help you enter the circles you desire to be in, disrupt the ones you want to conquer, or to start your own. The world eventually gets bored with the same thing from the same people. Though they are not interested in doing something different themselves, they'll pay for whoever does. Knowing this valuable secret, you must remain steadfast in doing what others won't do. The influential, the wealthy and the powerful all had to do it. Networking provides you with a complimentary GPS to do it also, with brand new routes, strategic fast lanes and unlimited global fuel. You are one connection away from arriving at all of your destinations. Now go put these keys in your networking ignition and drive baby drive.

Thoughts from Portugal

"Networking is a way of life, it is a life credo! It is the crucial fuel that drives development of personal and business projects in the XXI century. Without it life would be boring and it would be much more difficult to accomplish your goals. When someone asks for help I normally answer that the only reason not to do it is if I cannot. When someone has the courage to seek for help, one should be available as others are to us. It is always an opportunity to know better individuals and learn from them."
-João Diogo Ramos, CEO at Retmarker,
Founder at Collectors Bridge

Advice from Fiji

"There are few moments in life when we throw ourselves feet first, fearfully and curiously anticipating change. Networking is the game-changer."

-Keasi Tora, Logistics & Development Manager

GERMAINE MOODY

MORE THOUGHTS, SUCCESS AND ADVICE FROM GLOBAL CONTRIBUTORS

Success from Andorra

"My first real sales experience, 19 years old, selling encyclopedias for the Enterprise Artecrom in Spain, with very little knowledge of the Spanish language at that time. Just entered a customs office and asked for Juan (as 80% of the boys in Andalusia are named Juan). Just did if I had known Juan for a few years and managed to speak to him under 4 eyes. He laughed a lot when I explained to him my sales strategy and bought me some products. I did not leave after but asked him to recommend me to his colleagues and he did. Almost all of them bought me something (from encyclopedia to lithographs). Before leaving the office with a stunning sales result I also asked all his colleagues to write me down 1 or more names of friends, family and colleagues. This whole week my sales was based on their recommendations and with huge results! Of course this only happens when you manage to gain their sympathy, and your products/services are remarkable."

-Bianca Meeuwissen, General Mgr.,
My World Of Experiences

Thoughts from Azerbaijan

"As I'm a freelancer and do not spend money on self-marketing, the most part of all my business projects comes to me from my network - friends, relatives, past colleagues and their business contacts."

-Gurban Dashdamirov, Professional Marketer

Success from Bangladesh

"I got an opportunity to work for SD Asia (sdasia.co) which is regarded as one of the few platforms for entrepreneurs and freelancers in our context of Bangladesh. This was made possible due to my network I developed through sharing my works on social media. Since my experiences in managing events successfully while studying at University helped me position myself in promising networks, I always believed networking as the driving factor for creating opportunities to explore my creative potentials. This is how networking in relevant sector gave me a startup much needed for my career progression."

-Imtiaj Nasir, Broadcast Journalist & Filmmaker

Advice from Belgium

"WHAT you know can definitely be a determining factor in your future success, but more importantly is WHO you know. Being inspired, motivated and gaining valuable insights through face-to-face conversations where people can leverage each other's knowledge, experience and network. Networking leads towards co-creation, collaboration and innovation where people are complimentary towards each other, because every person is unique!"

-Vic Vanhove, Start-Up Consultant

Success from Bolivia

"A big part of the growth of my ecommerce brand (Flux Chargers) was due to the relationships we built by networking with several writers that later were willing to feature our company in the media outlets that they contribute to. Thanks to the 50+ media features that we received (such as Huffington Post, Mashable and Engadget) we grew our ecommerce brand by 1500% in one year alone."

-Alejandro Rioja, CEO and Founder of Flux Ventures LLC

Thoughts from Botswana

"As an education developer it has been amazing to travel to a place then be able to go back home and continue communicating as if I never left. Teaching and training for me has taken on a new life with the development of technology. Although there are a lot of disadvantages, there are creative and inspiring advantages in technology. The ICanLearnProgram has been transforming the idea of how children and adults learn by connecting and networking our information through everything that connects us as people, from our lifestyle, to what we watch on television, to what and how we behave. Together with the idea of connecting the child or adult with their source of self; they then learn what they need to understand, and connect with others. Networking then becomes the key that is combined with information technology to help that child or adult feel understood in their style of learning, through instant gratification, positive affirmation and resonated connections to ideas. Once the idea is initiated the continued development can be maintained and transformed further through communication and networking."

-Jillian Mary Sigamoney, Founder IcanLearnProgram

Thoughts from Canada

"Networking positions us to be found by those who are seeking our brilliance to improve their lives and businesses."

-Michele Hanson-O'Reggio, Business Leverage Expert

Thoughts from Canada

"Despite all the sophisticated tools and gadgets, people still use raw emotions to do business. Networking is the vehicle for our emotions, and trust is the destination."

-Adel C. Hammoud, Job Developer & Facilitator

Advice from Canada

"Be honest and try to help people you meet solve problems that trouble them. Make it more about them than you. Develop long lasting friendships that benefit everyone."
-Ian Herbert, CEO and President of Ian's Contracting

Advice from Canada

"Social media is only one aspect of networking, meeting face to face is crucial. The most important thing to do is lose the fear. Yes there is an etiquette to networking, and you will learn that as you go, but the most important aspect of networking, is, like everything else: Just show up!"
-George Fiala, President, Brainwerx Group, Executive Search (IT and Finance)

Thoughts from Canada

"I am an accessible travel specialist and my focus is on creating inclusion globally. I have MS (multiple sclerosis) and the comfort of creating conversations via social media on a global scale replaces the 'walk around the room' form of networking. I chime in to Twitter chats, post relevantly on LinkedIn and Skype with professionals around the world."
-Tarita Karsanji-Davenock, CEO Travel For All

Success from Chile

"Currently I am working on creating a center of open innovation oriented to enterprises and entrepreneurs. I've recruited the core team just based on my personal network, with the participation of professionals in San Francisco, Barcelona, London, Montevideo and Santiago de Chile. The experience was fantastic thanks to the chemistry that has occurred among all team members, the desire to share, network, to learn and to contribute to a cause that aims to make a contribution to society."
-Luis Cuezzo, Founder, Digital Glue

Success from Comoros

"I was helped by an American woman that I met in a networking session, to write a project that is now impacting thousands of people. Without networking, none of this would have been possible."
-Tourki Mohamed Ali, Student

Success from Democratic Republic Of The Congo

"Networking helped me develop the background of my insurance company to be launched in less than two months. Through networking, I was able to get the right people and partners during the creation of the company."
-Baraka Pilipili, Founder and CEO, CEFRADI Group

Advice from Cook Islands

"Use networking to advance your life and to live as much as possible."
-Augustine Kopa, Cook Islands Sports and National Olympic Committee

Advice from Croatia

"When networking, be honest and nice to all people, not just to those you think are successful and that could help you in your career."
-Igor Bartolic, Network Consultant

Thoughts from Cyprus

"Networking allows you to connect with people and get to know more cultures. Through the communication and knowledge you gain, you become a greater person. If your network is big and growing, you'll have more advantages and opportunities."
-Andreas Photiou, Software Developer,
Cooperative Computer Society Ltd

Advice from Denmark

"Nobody is an island, and in this digital information age, making the world both bigger & smaller by the day, one need to rely on networking and knowledge sharing."

-Tina Jonasen, Social Business Advisor at ThinkInNewAreas and Female Courage Foundation

Success from Denmark

"I was negotiating with a client for months about signing a deal with our company and couldn't get through. Coincidently, we were attending the same conference and managed to network there and signed the deal the following week."

-Faizan Syed, Digital Marketing Advisor

Advice from Djibouti

"Pay attention to the educational aspect and real value of networking. Organize face-to-face interactive discussions, this will be very beneficial to the future of everyone."

-Ismail Osman Ahmed, Governmental Organization

Thoughts from Gambia

"Networking is an effective way to build business partners and clients as well as acquire new knowledge and skills."

-Modou Njie, CEO/Entrepreneur

Thoughts from Germany

"Generations are in these days very much defined by their approach to and usage of technologies. These technologies have brought digital communication and with them new collaboration and networking methods that partly replace, partly complement traditional methods. I wish for all generations of networkers to always try to connect across these at times fundamental borders and therefore be able to benefit from knowledge and skills of their own and of other generations."

-Rene Wetzel, Online Marketing Executive at MBD.berlin

Thoughts from Ghana

"No man is an Island, we have to link up with each other, by building bridges to connect up, but not walls to limit people."
-Evans Kyeremeh, Radio Host

Success from Gibraltar

"Thanks to networking, I was able to start a soccer team from scratch and we're now competing at top European level."
-Albert Parody, Founder and President Lynx FC

Thoughts from Guatemala

"Networking is pivotal to increasing your opportunities for new experiences, encountering people from different walks of life and industries."
-Luis Alejos, Writer/Artist

Success from Guyana

"Me completing my MBA was due to building a really great network. Several of my colleagues were business students while I was more into diplomacy and international relations. Networking with them give me a wider spectrum of knowledge of business and how the theory in the textbooks works in practical, which led me to finish my studies based on knowledge I gained from their experience."
-Delon Fraser, Armed Forces

Advice from Iceland

"Share information. Reply to all and be friendly even though there is nothing in it for you."
-Thorunn Reynisdottir, CEO

Thoughts from Jamaica

"Networking is crucial for building and maintaining sustainable and long lasting relationships. Human beings cannot survive without local and international relationships."
-Aubryn Smith, Lecturer in Statistics Vector Technology Institute

Success from Liechtenstein

"Since 2004 in Estonia I lead the developing and realization of my/our interdisciplinary artistic work in progress project (a kind of a never ending story). Until now we were active with the project in eight European countries: Estonia, Serbia, Bosnia and Herzegovina, Principality of Liechtenstein, Croatia, Slovakia, Slovenia and Italy. Without the investment of the energy in the building of my network and without the activities and assistance from my network, I could do nothing."

-Vlado Franjević, Project Leader and Author

Success from Lithuania

"Thanks to networking, I have created the Lithuanian Contacts Network (10,000 members) which has been a tremendous source of business for me."

-Romualdas Maciulis, Consultant and Professional Speaker

Thoughts from Madagascar

"Today, the way of working is rather in the dematerialization and sharing. This phenomenon is not only widespread but today especially profitable. The networking allows in-progress in a consistent manner with the other and tendencies, which was my case when creating my company."

-Miary Andrianosy, Manager/Owner of
MYKANDRA Useful Technology

Success from Nepal

"The women trekking guide in Nepal was a nightmare when we started in 90'. Nepal is a patriarchal society, having gender inequality in the entire job market. The locals community were suspicious and against our work to involve Nepalese women in the trekking industry. Though, we were in the global network through tourism which helped us to establish a new profession for the Nepalese women. Even all our society was against us but the

tourists appreciated our initiation, recommending their friends and family to cooperate with our women empowerment mission. Now, this is one of the most innovative professions for many rural and disadvantaged women to work as a trekking guide. Now, this profession is well established in Nepali society and thanks to networking, also globally, replicating in many different countries."
-Lucky K. Chhetri, 3 Sisters Adventure Trekking

Advice from Poland

"Go out so you can meet someone. Learn languages so you are able to communicate, learn how to communicate so they understand you, listen and understand what others want to say, in order to enrich your life and the life of others."
-Martin David, AML Analyst at Citibank

Success from Somalia

"When I founded SomLite (sustainable energy company that focuses off-grid rural somalis) I didn't have a clear vision on how to scale up and grow the company. By networking, I met interesting people and mentors who have guided me to bring SomLite to next level."
-Abdishakur Ahmed, Co-Founder & CEO

Success from South Africa

"Through networking, I was able to build a phenomenal team of like-minded individuals of more than 800 people in 7 months with our company."
-Esteban Smit, Diamond Director at Mema

Advice from South Africa

"My advice to future networkers is to build yourself a network from as young as possible and also find a mentor."
-Mike Herbig, CEO, Network Marketer

Thoughts from Spain

"Networking is a huge opportunity to experience new people, employers, coworkers, clients and friends. It allows you to learn and share new knowledge."
-*Eloisa Oliva, Account Mgr., FX Specialist*

Thoughts from Spain

"All my work is done by networking. I started doing what I'm doing by networking. The best friend of my cousin let me in his SEO team. SEO was a new market and all the knowledge was shared by contacts. You grow and help to grow others."
-*Carlos Fernandez, Digital Marketer*

Success from Swaziland

"Networking has allowed me to interact with like-minded beings who share some of the same common interests and goals that I have. This not only provides encouragement for me but also more opportunities."
-*Sicelo Mkhuleko Hlophe, Technical Sales Rep.*

Advice from Sweden

"My advice to future networkers is to take advantage of the biggest net of all time, the internet."
-*Lisa Mattsson, Asst. to Investment Advisors*

Advice from Switzerland

"Be positive, likeable and unforgettable. Approach people gingerly and listen to what they have to say. Provide a snazzy business card with a strapline of what you do and how that can make your contacts' lives better."
-*Anne Liebgott, CEO, Where Americans are Welcome*

Thoughts from Taiwan

"Respect people and everything on earth and in the universe. You then will have the natural smile and the best resources and

connections from all parties. It's all about networking now. The future is now, the future is networking."
-Ed Yen, CO-Founder GCA Entertainment, COO Arts & Fashion Center

Success from Turkey
"I networked my way to Turkey and I'm now a General Manager with a construction company, plus I've started my own LTD Company."
-Volkan Mahmut Daglilar, GM Sales and Marketing

Success from Uganda
"A big portion of my life is made up of friends and my friends come from networking."
-Kintu Andrew, Business Development Director Simcom Engineering

Success from Ukraine
"Networking has allowed me to meet a lot of amazing people (including Germaine) who continue to help me understand what the world wants from me and how I can contribute to it. It's helped me to regularize my thoughts and has changed my life."
-Alexandr Okonechnikov, Founder Nuts & Fruits

Success from United Kingdom
"I owe many thanks to networking. Most significantly, coming from a very poor background in a small village in Africa to setting up my own business in Europe."
-Susan Idama, Fashion Designer & CEO

Advice from United Kingdom
"If you limit yourself to only your close colleagues and friends, you do just that, 'limit yourself'! In today's ever more barrier-less world, networking not just locally, but outside your regional and business sphere can bring dividends across your career from

opportunities you would never have encountered. These come from enriching your knowledge and experience to monetary opportunities. A great deal of 'own luck' can be created by networking and engaging in areas that interest you and you have knowledge and opinion on. Put yourself out there, but don't expect immediate benefit as you need to work at it."
-Ian Moyse, Board Member Eurocloud

Thoughts from United Kingdom
"As the saying goes "it's not what you know, it's who you know." The power of networking is to connect with people who you choose to bring into your circles of influence. It is in those circles where opportunities flourish. With unemployment being at a high, employers look for people they know, the same is true in forming business partnerships. Reach out and connect with people, build the relationships, and opportunities will come your way."
-Richard Craig, Founder/Partner Empowering Events

Success from United Kingdom
"Organizing the annual event for women of color would not have taken place for three years without successful networking, as speakers, and attendees alike came from successful networking."
-Lillian Ogbogoh, TV Host and Presenter

Advice from United Kingdom
"If you have never been to a networking event, accompany a friend/colleague/contact who is a seasoned networker. If you attend a new networking group alone, ask the organisers to introduce you to a few people. Ask questions and really listen to the answers, repeat back to the person so they know you understood and are listening. Build connections to refer people to - become the 'go-to' person for something specific. Give back wherever possible either by helping out at an event or promoting events via your Website, Newsletter and Social Media."
-Rachel Gedney, Partner Empowering Events

Advice from United Kingdom

"The more you put into networking, the more you get out. Look to be as helpful and supportive as you can to the people you meet. Ask not what your network can do for you, but what you can do for your network. If everyone else follows this approach then the net benefit will be significant, if they don't then you will be the most helpful relationship for the people in your network. Both outcomes are good for you."

-Piers Wilson, Head of Product Management, Huntsman Security

Thoughts from United States Of America

"Networking makes the dream work. Only you can do it, but you can't do it alone. Through networking you build relations and attract success partners. All successful people have had a mastermind group behind them. They found them through networking. So can you."

-Steven Gans, CEO AB Consulting LLC

Advice from United States Of America

"As a bit of an introvert, I had to work hard to become comfortable with networking. Finding the best networking tactics that work for you is worth it. Identify your strengths (and play off them), and your weaknesses (and improve them). Push yourself, walk up to people, and truly listen. Also, don't focus on networking only with the big dogs—networking with every single person, whether it's a secretary or business owner, can deliver surprising results. You never know who is connected to who."

-Lauren Wise, Founder/Head of Editorial of Midnight Publishing

Advice from United States Of America

"Don't spread yourself too thin. Trust your gut when meeting and relating to people. Seek first how you may serve. Become a valuable free resource."

-Elizabeth Houser, Account Executive

Thoughts from United States Of America

"Networking is the only way to create lasting change, have a positive impact, leave a legacy and perpetually shift the paradigm as we know it."

-Eric Montross, Founder Leadership Mindset Network

Success from United States Of America

"I created an internet advertising company by assembling a team from a network I established while working for a company in the same space. Now I lead a company that competes with my former employer in a harmonious way. In Silicon Valley, we call it "Coopetition". It is the concept that we all Cooperate and Compete with each other. By establishing alliances on specific topics with a network, all parties win."

-Michael Miller, President, Becker Interactive, Inc.

Success from United States Of America

"I became the CEO of an exciting technology company because of my network. I was able to grow the revenue and profits of that company very successfully thanks to many people in my network and resulted in selling the company for a very large multiple after only 12 months in the job. The key to success in any endeavor is the ability to get things done. The better networked you are, the more people you can draw on to help you get things done and the faster you will get things done. Time is the one resource you can never get more of and a quality network enables you to move your initiatives forward faster - short circuiting possibly many steps in making your ventures successful."

-Fred Thiel, Chairman & CEO Local Corporation

Advice from United States Of America

"Be authentic and come from a giving standpoint. When you are 100% real about what you are doing the RIGHT people come across your path. You align with like-minded individuals. When you are giving and seek outside of yourself on how you can help

others, you naturally put yourself in a space of also receiving!"
-Jaimi Alexander, Just Jaimi, LLC

Success from United States Of America

"Thanks to networking, I built a startup company from -0- to a Ranking of 71st of the 500 fastest growing companies in the United States."
-Jerry Muszynski, Executive VP Global Business Beyond Borders, LLC.

Thoughts from United States Of America

"Networking is the basis of the human experience, building relationships".
-Roddrick Bowers, Founder & CEO of Good News America 365

Thoughts from United States Of America

"Get off your phones and iPads, get out there and meet real people. Making a real connection is key."
-Michelle Arbeau, CEO of Authentic You Media

Advice from United States Of America

"Be generous. Be generous with your listening, your contacts, and your resources. The law of reciprocity will see to it that people are generous with you."
-Chad Murray, President, Your Credit Coach, LLC

Advice from United States Of America

"Slow down, make real connections, face to face-whether that be by Skype or in person. Take the time to establish a real human connection with people."
-Sharon Shores, Social Media Consultant

Thoughts from United States Of America

"Networking is the only opportunity to inform others of your passion, goods and/or services without paying for it. You are able

to find numerous connections that will allow you to assist others in growing their businesses in a collaborative environment. Be open to possibilities and outside of the box experiences. You never know who you will interact with and who will become an ally."
-Nan Arnstein, CEO/Founder of
Creative Arts for Developing Minds

Advice from United States Of America

"Be creative and keep your contacts organized, updated and replicated. Continuously seek out individuals that are good at what they do, people you can learn from. Even if someone isn't able to plug you into an opportunity immediately, still be sure to maintain contact in any and every way possible by reaching out to them every now and again. As time unfolds, some of your most valuable assistance may arrive from the most unexpected of people and/or places."
-Derek Callaway, Independent Digital Security Consultant

Success from United States Of America

"Networking played a major part of my family's successful migration and recovery from the aftermath and devastation of Hurricane Katrina. We traveled to Tallahassee, FL a year prior to the storm for a leadership conference, where we met some really amazing people! Following the conference, we kept in touch on a slightly regular basis. One week after the storm, I was contacted by these same people who invited us to move to Tallahassee and to bunk with them for as long as we needed to. We lived with them for 1 1/2 months, and as a result, my family has since recovered and are well on our way to pursuing our dreams and achieving our goals in music and entertainment. We also gained some wonderful friends for life as a result of networking."
-Reginald Joseph, CEO/President at Red J Entertainment

Thoughts from United States Of America

"Networking says you are serious about raising awareness about your brand as well as connecting with others whose time you value. Networking isn't about collecting a bunch of business cards, but rather building meaningful relationships with those who you want to see succeed. When I first began my journey into public speaking, I didn't have a very strong contact list; no one would hire me. It wasn't until I joined a mastermind that a woman whom I had become friends with put me in contact with a local university that gave me my first opportunity to speak. Networking had truly worked!"

-Wilda Nubia, Speaker

Advice from United States Of America

"Write a thank you note to everyone who is gracious enough to offer you a business card or a piece of advice to you. Ask others what you can do for them or what they are looking for in their business, you want to be a contribution as often as possible. People will remember you and can become a valuable resource when you are in search of something or someone that will propel your business or project. Ask for permission if you are going to pass someone's name or service along to another connection - this demonstrates respect and appreciation of their time and talents. Show gratitude and appreciation to the special people in your life publicly - it shows you are human and your team matters."

-Janet Edwards, President and CEO, Paving the Way

Thoughts from United States Of America

"The relationships we build with people determines our success or failure in life - and the ease or difficulty with which we attain success. If we don't learn how to develop and maintain positive connections, we almost certainly guarantee hardships and struggles on our journeys. Also, no one person knows everything. We all have our limitations. Having a network (and an open mind) helps to fill in the gaps in our skills and knowledge. It gives us an opportunity to share and gain knowledge and resources in order to create a culture of success."

-Eric Foster, Founder and Editor-in-Chief of YBE Magazine

Thoughts from United States Of America

"Networking is important because it is a bridge that can take us to any part of the world."

-Derrick Hayes, Encouragement Speaker

Success from United States Of America

"At Book Expo, the largest industry conference for publishing professionals, I actively engaged a publisher of health care books. Our interaction that day secured seven book projects during a span of two years. That was the ultimate networking outcome for a contract editor! Proactive networking can show instant credibility because you present such an organic snapshot of who you are and what you offer. It is a test of your communication skills, professionalism, appearance, personality, demonstration of genuine concern for someone's needs that your services may match, and so much more that can set you apart from any competitor in your field."

-Candi S. Cross, Ghostwriter and Editor

Thoughts from United States Of America

"Networking is communication at its finest. It is about connecting to the heart, mind and soul of the individual. When a true network has been established it is a thread that cannot be broken by time, circumstances or people; that is why it is imperative to continue to search for those hearts, minds and souls that were once connected and are now re-establishing their bonds."

-Yvonne Gamble, CEO Simplified Knowledge, Exec. Dir. Women Leading Change Now

Thoughts from United States Of America

"Networking is as essential to humans as water is to fish. Not a single soul lives alone in this world, and none were intended to be alone. We were all created for fellowship with our Creator and each other. Through this unspoken mutuality of purpose, each of us through networking, can grow not only in opportunity, but be enriched, strengthened, and helped when necessary to find the courage, support and strength necessary to reach our goals and dreams together, where alone we would be without hope and ultimately become void of meaning or purpose. Establishing and involving yourself in professional and personal relationships with particular people in particular communities will change you: and not only will you internalize a variety of interesting points of view, but will allow you a wider, more understanding, accepting and appreciative view of how our differences individually, make us better people wholly and universally."

-Lisa R. Terry, CEO Terry Advisory Group

Success from United States Of America

"By networking through a local chamber of commerce I joined and volunteering to conduct an early morning workshop, I met one of my best coaching clients. But the result was not immediate. I conducted a workshop on Diversity. Two or three years later, a business owner called the chamber to see if they had anyone who worked in the area of diversity. They gave her my information and we have worked together off and on for over 5 years."

-Rachel Elahee, Psychologist, Certified Life Coach, & Author

Thoughts from United States Of America

"I believe you get what you give in this world. That is my motto. If you are able to connect people together that can be helpful to one another, I believe the Universe rewards you for the effort. The most valuable thing you have in this life is your relationships and your network's willingness to make a "credible vouch" on your behalf."

-Sean Lyons, Founder of Triad Real Estate Partners

Thoughts from United States Of America

"Business is done based on relationships, and the most effective, the most powerful and the easiest way to build relationships is through networking. We like to work with people we know and trust or people referred to us by people we know and trust. Networking is our entrée to meet those people."

-Lillian Bjorseth, Networking & Communication Skills Speaker

Success from United States Of America

"Being referred into and recommended as a national speaker for the Office of the Sect of Defense in the Yellow Ribbon program was made possible through networking, and mostly everything that I have accomplished has been through the same support and help of others."

-Ron Sukenick, Founder Relationship Strategies Institute

Advice from United States Of America

"Be aware of your surroundings and understand with what you are dealing. Ask questions, share ideas, stories and successes. Be yourself, connect with those who are in different spaces than your chosen profession, use your resources and offer up yours. Use grace, be grateful and always remain humble."

-Stephanie M. Gilbert, Sr. Talent Acquisition Partner Caas

Thoughts from United States Of America

"Networking allows an individual to increase their territory. The more people you meet, the more opportunities become possible. Another great part of networking is having spokespeople. If your encounter is awesome, or impressive, people will speak highly of you to their most intimate circles."

-Gregory Meriweather, CEO Black on Black Network

Advice from United States Of America

"You should always try to see things in an open minded thought process while growing your network. As you choose networks to

grow with be sure that your network follows your heart tug or get out and find another one as the saying goes there are plenty of fish in the sea the same holds true for groups."
-Lisa Neppel Danzer, Co-Founder EvolveUS.Org

Thoughts from United States Of America

"Networking produces an instant collaboration of skills, enhances opportunity while building relationships and creating repositories for current and future use."
-Shawn Eadens, Chief Information Officer JLA Consulting

Advice from United States Of America

"Be open to new opportunities that present themselves and be prepared for the unexpected. Networking is a two-way street, be sure to reciprocate with your contacts. Networking can happen anyplace at anytime. Online, in the workplace, the classroom, the subway station, or the grocery at 2:00 a.m. It can happen anywhere!"
-James Atkinson, Higher Education and Organization Development Strategist

Advice from United States Of America

"Be genuine and specific. Provide benefit to those that you network with. Be appropriate in the presentation of yourself, making a good first impression. Never become intoxicated at a networking event. Take notes for action later, and be clear that the notes are for you to follow through."
-William E. Higgins Jr., Founder Semper Resurgam

Thoughts from United States Of America

"The future belongs to the networker, the connector, the collaborator. There are many reasons for this, but prominent among them is the fact that increasingly, insight rather than information, and wisdom, rather than knowledge, is where advantage lies. And groundbreaking, game-changing insight most

often lies at the intersection between people, groups, cultures, and cosmologies. Our current era is marked by the convergence of technological, cultural and economic trends that accelerate connectedness, and magnify the advantages of connectedness. In such an era, the skill of networking and the culture of networking, is not just a "nice to have", it's a must have."
-Gogo Erekosima, President & Founder Idea Age Consulting

Success from United States Of America

"My company was built through networking and by my network. Closed mouths do not get fed; get out there and do it, don't be afraid of a "no"; think big, dream bigger, execute."
-Yakov Elizarov, State of Maryland Business and Economic Development Rep. to Eurasia

Success from United States Of America

"I'm a professional speaker, and in fall 2014, I was invited to give an inspirational speech at an employee leadership awards luncheon at a corporation ranked in the top 10 of the Fortune 500. I tried to create opportunities to speak/train at this company for 2 years. However, I networked with a fellow Northwestern University alum last summer. She is a senior-level executive at the company, and she graciously opened the door by recommending me as a speaker. Two years worth of hard work to gain access was erased with one networking connection!"
-Rachelle Smith, Principal & Founder of Positive Creative Infusion Consulting

Advice from United States Of America

"Make networking a priority; know that it takes time and be willing to set aside time specifically for helping others by networking. Don't overcommit; if you are unable to help someone, because of time or lack of experience in a given subject, then be up front quickly and don't try to help someone for the sake of it - it

will help them and you. Temper your expectations; not everyone has the same ethic of networking, and may expect something in return or claim that you will owe them a favor. Be persistent; continually find opportunities to help others, broaden your network and knowledge base, and realize there can be many steps in the process to get to a key decision maker."
-*Douglas Duesing, Key Account Manager Caterpiller*

Advice from United States Of America
"Be intentional in your networking activities and know that it takes work. Rome was not built in a day and neither will your network. Remember, that the key to networking is relationship building."
-*Augusta Massey, Principal Attorney*
Massey & Associates Law Firm

Success from United States Of America
"When I was a new nurse I knew I wanted to specialize in open heart recovery. The hospital I was working in had just started a program, but they only wanted to transfer in/hire nurses with open heart recovery skills. A few weeks later, I was at a conference and attending a networking session. I mentioned my goals to a colleague who told me about an opportunity at her hospital. She was able to get me an interview and the rest was up to me."
-*Liz Fackina, Director Value Analysis,*
NYU Langone Medical Center

Thoughts from United States Of America
"Network, network, network and not limit your efforts just to a particular niche as you never know the vastness of a new connections network. Successful people don't become successful by trying to go it alone, but rather connecting with successful people in a mutually beneficial way -- like a joint venture -- and utilizing not only their knowledge but their established network to build your credibility and platform."
-*William Constantine, CEO at William Constantine International*

Advice from United States Of America

"Be aggressive. Put yourself out there in every way possible and be persistent. Networking is all a numbers game and the more prepared you are and the more people you reach out to the better the results will be. Developing this skill is one of the most important skills you can have as no one can be successful without a little help from others."

-David Perlman, Managing Director of Iron Consulting & Staffing

Thoughts from United States Of America

"Networking is the first step in brand recognition. Your attitude and elevator pitch let's people know if they have any true interest in you."

-Richard O'Malley, Event Producer,
President of The O'Malley Project

Thoughts from United States Of America

"People call it networking, I call it connecting and fostering relationships on another plane. Relationships can be built on our commonalities or our differences and the appeal of both. Since I was a child, I enjoyed learning about people and with each fascinating story I wanted my family and friends to meet them as well. I've always "networked" and still connect to people from my childhood and have had the pleasure of expanding on our commonalities by working together and sharing our unique different skillsets to all of our benefit."

-Carmen M. Colon, Author and Social Media Marketing Consultant

Advice from United States Of America

"Open your heart and be specific in your desired and intentional outcome. Allow your brain to work it's natural magic and create a network simply by talking about your thoughts/goals/intentions with everyone. Being positive and trying to see with a real lens the 'why' and the 'how' will propel people to want to join you to help

create bodacious outcomes. When you commit with pure intention to create positive change in our world, and take action, people will come together and you'll never be without community, a greatest benefit of networking."
-Susan L. Axelrod, Philanthropy Advisor Axelrod Philanthropy Advising and Confident Fundraising

Success from United States Of America

"As someone who is closing in on retirement age, but will not retire, 90% of the work I have done successfully has been due to networking. Credit goes to people I know for their help."
-David L. Morehead, Executive Director at Calling From The Dream

Advice from United States Of America

"Be open minded, know your brand, understand the right way of selling and the wrong way of selling. It is all marketing your brand and sharing the passion in what you do and how you deliver yourself."
-Ayeesha S. Kanji, Owner ASK.Solutions

Advice from United States Of America

"Let networking become 2nd nature to you. When you're at a school function, talk with other parents, when you take the dog to the dog park, talk to the other people there, you already share a common interest, (dogs), and you never know who you're gonna meet that you might be able to network with in the future. Any social situation is an opportunity to network, even if it's just introducing yourself and asking what they do for a living, you never know where it could lead."
-Marie DeWolfe, CEO, Journalist & Blogger Dixieland Media

Success from United States Of America

"Through networking, I have been able to implement a system that will help youth turn their roadblocks into building blocks throughout Northeast Ohio."
-Cedric Brown, Founder & CEO of U Can SOAR

Thoughts from United States Of America

"We have an incredible opportunity to join hands with others around the world as we share in an exchange of thoughts, goals, and perceptions. We can learn and commiserate from others to improve our lives and, perhaps, ease the burden of others. Thanks to networking, we are never alone."

-Mary Frances Fisher, Legal Nurse Consultant

Advice from United States Of America

"Know what you want from a networking opportunity ahead of time. Be specific and intentional for your networking goal. Listen more than you talk. Take plenty of business cards. Relax and have fun!"

-Bob Pierce, Co-Founder and Mentor

Thoughts from United States Of America

"It is the only way to really connect in today's world. We may have technology, but it is only a means to a true networking opportunity. Today's job market is so competitive that job seekers, career changers and ordinary folks looking for connections, have to engage in some type of networking to achieve goals."

-Gary Hines, President, The Gary Hines Consulting Group

Advice from United States Of America

"Perseverance is the key word, don't give up easily, if you do you will miss the opportunities that networking has for you. Finally, after you network do business with integrity, loyalty and transparency, with that you will always achieve success."

-Gisela De Jesus, Managing Partner and Co-Founder

Advice from United States Of America

"Establish yourself as a thought-leader in your field of expertise, operate with integrity at all times, On your journey...the good, bad and ugly, while seeking to acknowledge and embrace greatness recognized in others. Reputation management is key to obtaining

success within the digital arena, while character building and revealing is equally important to the initial process for the making of an empire through networking. Build your platform for more than one through impartation of ideas turned reality. This in turn will duplicate your efforts by multiplication...enlarging your territory...empowering your message...developing people."
-Sherri Henley, Founder and CEO Business Over Coffee International

Thoughts from United States Of America

"We can't build a successful empire without surrounding ourselves with like-minded people. Sometimes those like-minded people are not in your immediate circle of influence. More power is produced when two or more like-minded people strategize on a common issue. And it is a way of working smarter and not harder."
-Tangela Days, Founder of Discovering Me, The MasterPiece

Success from United States Of America

"One of my biggest successes with networking is not about me per say, but about my student. I am a business instructor at a local community college. Each month I attend the local chamber of commerce jobs program, and I invite my classes. On this instance I had only one student to attend. She was from South Korea and had been in the US for about 3 years working. I introduced her to the vice president of the chamber who immediately spoke to her in Korean. They hit it off. The vice president then introduced her to other members, one of which was president of a company that was extending their company to South Korea. This student now works for that company, gets to go home at least twice a year for business. You never know who you are going to meet, and what may come out of it."
-Maricia Johns, Blogger "This Is Your Best Year"

Thoughts from United States Of America
"Networking is the shortest path to influencers. In other words, networking accelerates success by reaching contacts through strategic partners that would have otherwise taken you much longer to reach on your own. For example, many big deals have been struck simply by networking over cocktails or on the golf course. Only through networking has it been possible for me to meet State Reps, top sales trainers, CEO's, millionaires and share the stage with a top motivational speaker."
-Robert E. Reed, Personal Branding Strategist

Success from United States Of America
"Through networking I was given the opportunity to make a presentation to a group of people who were very interested in my topic (health and wellness, in particular dietary chemical cleanup). The presentation went very well, I connected with a number of people at the event, sold some books, got some newsletter subscribers. One year later I received a phone call from a major national corporation and wound up doing a series of health and wellness lectures for them. From the initial contact to the presentation to the lecture series was approximately 18 months. You have to be patient."
-Mira Dessy, Nutrition Educator at Grains & More,
The Ingredient Guru

Thoughts from United States Of America
"In this world of increasing technology, people often underestimate the power of offline marketing. Connecting face-to-face has not and will not lose its power and its place in business and society. We connect with people and trust people more (and are more willing to buy from) who we know or have met in person."
-Lisa Starr, CEO of Starr Global Enterprises

Thoughts from United States Of America

"Networking is the lifeline to any business because without connecting with others it is nearly impossible to further your dreams. Connecting with others through networking is the key to success."

-Lorraine Grant, Owner/CEO

Advice from United States Of America

"Be an engaged and active listener. Focus your energy and attention towards making connections with others who share your interests and passions, but find ways to mix it up a bit too. Remember networking is a two-way exchange, find ways to give as well as receive. Build a diverse network, in age, ethnicity, and social standing. When looking for mentors keep in mind experience and expertise comes in all ages and walks of life."

-Ellanor Smith, Project Mgmt. Professional

GERMAINE MOODY

15 WORDS THAT MATTER THE MOST

We asked our global contributors to tell us one word that matters the most for someone to become a successful networker. We accumulated a total of 216 words from all over the world. Below are the Top 15 in alphabetical order that matter the most when networking.

AUTHENTICITY - Your uniqueness and authenticity is what separates you from the global networking crowd. Always be authentic and never be afraid to be your amazing self.

BELIEVE - You need to have belief in yourself and belief that you will be successful in what you are pursuing, not afraid or fearful to use every resource for networking.

COMMUNICATE - Your communication skills play a significant role in your networking. Your ability to listen, express yourself with clarity and communicate with a diverse group of people is key to scaling your network.

GIVE - The world is drawn to networkers who are givers, those who are constantly giving of themselves via their talents, their knowledge, their motivation, their time, their joy and their wisdom in order to help someone else.

HONESTY - Honesty really is the best policy, simply because trust is everything when it comes to networking or any type of

onship (business, personal, friends, etc). Honesty
enhances transparency, which is a magnet to gain followers and
supporters.

INTEGRITY - Say what you mean, mean what you say, do
what you said you're going to do. Don't try to be something or
agree with anything that goes against what you believe as truth
for yourself. Integrity will always separate you from the crowd
in networking and in life.

LISTEN - If you have a problem with listening, you will have
problems for the rest of your life. It is the same with
networking, it will amount to nothing. Practice listening,
master listening. Secrets, strategies and advantages are all
discovered by listening.

OPENNESS - The most connected networkers are normally
those who are more open to others and keep their options open
when it comes to their network. In order to influence the
masses and build a massive network, openness is mandatory.

PASSION - A true passion for people, for connecting, for
interacting, for expansion, for collaboration and for
communication, is what it takes to become a master networker.

PERSISTENCE - Be persistent in all of your networking.
Having a relentless determination is a must to make the
connections you desire and to get the deal or collaboration
you've dreamed of.

POSITIVITY - There's nothing more magnetic than a positive
networker. The most successful people in the world are also the
most positive when it comes to motivation. Use positivity to
your advantage everywhere.

SHARE - Master networkers are known to share advice, suggestions, ideas, referrals, connections, recommendations and more. Sharing enables you to build a massive network by being a helpful resource.

STRATEGY - Open networking is great but strategic networking is the best. If you have target connections then you should go after those, while remaining open to potential gatekeepers that can connect you as well. With the right networking strategy, you can achieve every goal.

TRUST - Trust is the doorway to opportunities within your network, their network and beyond. Once you establish trust, you establish access. With access, not only can you fulfill your dreams but you can also make dreams come true for others.

VALUE - What you bring to the table matters tremendously in networking. Most people will connect with you based solely on the value they perceive you can add to their life in some way. Several things can increase your value to others, but being a supporter and an encourager of those in your network will add the greatest value to your networking.

GERMAINE MOODY

LIST OF GLOBAL CONTRIBUTORS

ALBANIA - Armando Shkurti
ALGERIA - Karim Djerboa
ANDORRA - Bianca Meeuwissen
ANGOLA - Evandro José Coelho do Amaral
ARGENTINA - Rodrigo Borgia
ARMENIA - Gevorg Nersisyan
ARUBA - Richard Visser
AUSTRALIA - Tez Blackmore
AZERBAIJAN - Gurban Dashdamirov
BAHAMAS - Jerome G. Sherman
BAHRAIN - Abdulaziz Khattak
BANGLADESH - Imtiaj Nasir
BARBADOS - Gavin Robinson
BELGIUM - Sofiane Chami, Vic Vanhove
BELIZE - Joy Godfrey
BERMUDA - Arthur Rego
BHUTAN - Kezang, Om Nirola
BOLIVIA - Alejandro Rioja, Carla Doria-Medina
BOSNIA & HERZEGOVINA - Selma Sehic
BOTSWANA - Jillian Mary Sigamoney
BRAZIL - Pamela Granoff
BULGARIA - Sergey Petrov
BURKINA FASO - Harouna Timothée Kabore
BURUNDI - Niyongabo Felix
CAMBODIA - Kimiean Sreng

CAMEROON - Ndel-Andre Raoul
CANADA - Adel C. Hammoud, George Fiala, Ian Herbert, Laurie K. Grant, Michele Hanson-O'Reggio, Tarita Karsanji-Davenock
CAPE VERDE - Saidy Andrade
CHILE - Leonardo Nunes Ricucci, Luis Cuezzo
CHINA - Andrew S. Cheung
COLOMBIA - Alejandro Villada
COMOROS - Tourki Mohamed Ali
COOK ISLANDS - Augustine Kopa
COTE D'IVOIRE - Toti Jean Marc Yale
CROATIA - Goran Radic, Igor Bartolic
CURACAO - Margi Martinus
CYPRUS - Andreas Photiou
CZECH REPUBLIC - Gabriel Szalay
DEMOCRATIC REPUBLIC of the CONGO - Baraka Pilipili
DENMARK - Faizan Syed, Lynge Hansen, Tina Jonasen
DJIBOUTI - Ismail Osman Ahmed
DOMINICA - Cheryl Emanuel-Plummer
DOMINICAN REPUBLIC - Edison Sepúlveda
EGYPT - Shabbir Yamani
EQUATORIAL GUINEA - Manzo Mbomyo
ESTONIA - Olesija Saue
FIJI - Keasi Tora
FINLAND - Anne-Maria Yritys, Mikael Salo
FRANCE - Christophe Poizat, Ingrid Bouguenon
FRENCH GUINEA - Arne Horn
GAMBIA - Modou Njie
GEORGIA - Sandro Kipiani
GERMANY - Rene Wetzel, William Toll
GHANA - Evans Kyeremeh, Joseph Allotey-Kpakpoe, Noella Kisembo
GIBRALTAR - Albert Parody, Daniel Bula, James Richards
GREECE - Athanasios Batsakidis, Emmanuel Chrysis, Socratis Ploussas

GUAM - Vera Topasna
GUATEMALA - Luis Alejos
GUYANA - Carmilita Jamieson, Delon Fraser
HAITI - Laurent Hilaire
HONG KONG - Jay Kim
HUNGARY - Gabor Pinter
ICELAND - Thorunn Reynisdottir
INDIA - Raj Viswanadha
INDONESIA - Cahyana Purnama
IRAN - Abbas Hajifathali
IRELAND - Ogbeyalu Okoye
ISRAEL - Yasha Harari
ITALY - Carmine Cavaliere, Stefano Mongardi
JAMAICA - Anthony Wood, Aubryn Smith
JAPAN - Patricia Bader-Johnston
JORDAN - Mohammad Obaidat
KENYA - Julie Balcombe
LESOTHO - Ma-Lord T Mefane
LIECHTENSTEIN - Vlado Franjević
LITHUANIA - Donatas Jonikas, Romualdas Maciulis
LUXEMBOURG - Joanna Koleva
MADAGASCAR - Miary Andrianosy
MALAWI - Augustine Mumba
MALAYSIA - Oliver Kiet Wong
MALTA - Brian Role`
MAURITIUS - Suyash Sumaroo
MEXICO - Rodolfo Vega
MONTSERRAT - Warren Cassell
MOROCCO - Sassioui Zakaria
MOZAMBIQUE - Anissa Arune
MYANMAR - Anissa Arune
NEPAL - Lucky K. Chhetri
NETHERLANDS - Dave Klop
NEW ZEALAND - Chris Hanlon

NIGER - Ayouba Saley Souley
NIGERIA - Hussain AbdulQadir, Olushola Olaleye
OMAN - Donovan D. Rosenburg
PAKISTAN - Syed Irfan Ajmal
PALESTINE - Fatima Butmah
PANAMA - Sydney Tremayne
PERU - Mauricio Moya
PHILIPPINES - Angelica M. Baylon
POLAND - Martin David
PORTUGAL - João Diogo Ramos
QATAR - Mehul Indravadan Sheth
ROMANIA - Flavius Saracut
RWANDA - Uwumuremyi Jean Felix
SAINT VINCENT AND THE GRENADINES - Hayden Billingy
SAUDI ARABIA - Fahad Alkhorayef
SENEGAL - Ibrahima Kalil Kaba
SEYCHELLES - Nirmal Shah
SINGAPORE - John Chen
SLOVAK REPUBLIC - Martina Kičinová
SOMALIA - Abdishakur Ahmed, Yahya Mohamed Abdi
SOUTH AFRICA - Byron Nel, Esteban Smit, Mathew Daniel, Mike Herbig
SOUTH KOREA - Cristy Kim
SPAIN - Carlos Fernandez, Eloisa Oliva
SRI LANKA - Chamara Bandara
SURINAME - Ruth Sinkeler
SWAZILAND - Sicelo Mkhuleko Hlophe
SWEDEN - Lisa Mattsson
SWITZERLAND - Anne Liebgott
TAIWAN - Ed Yen, Jonathan Aufray
THAILAND - Norina Affiza
TRINIDAD & TOBAGO - Shayanne Friday
TURKEY - Volkan Mahmut-Daglilar
UGANDA - Kintu Andrew

UKRAINE - Alexandr Okonechnikov

UNITED KINGDOM - Ian Moyse, Lillian Ogbogoh, Piers Wilson, Rachel Gedney, Richard Craig, Susan Idama, Yannis Karipsiadis

UNITED STATES - Aaron Sims, Augusta Massey, Ayeesha Kanji, Bob Pierce, Candi Cross, Carmen Colon, Cedric Brown, Chad Murray, David Morehead, David Perlman, Derek Callaway, Derrick Hayes, Douglas Duesing, Elizabeth Houser, Ellanor Smith, Eric Foster, Eric Montross, Fred Thiel, Gary Hines, Gisela De Jesus, Gogo Erekosima, Gregory Meriweather, Jaimi Alexander, James Atkinson, Janet Edwards, Jerry Muszynski, John Vlcan, Lauren Wise, Lillian Bjorseth, Lisa Danzer, Lisa Starr, Lisa Terry, Liz Fackina, Lo Rene`, Marc Peurye, Maricia Johns, Marie DeWolfe, Mary Frances Fisher, Michael Miller, Michelle Arbeau, Mira Dessy, Monica Matthews, Nan Arnstein, Peter Roesler, Rachelle Smith, Reginald Joseph, Richard O'Malley, Robert Reed, Roddrick Bowers, Ron Sukenick, Sean Lyons, Sharon Shores, Shawn Eadens, Sherri Henley, Stephanie Gilbert, Steven Gans, Susan Axelrod, Tangela Days, Wilda Nubia, William Constantine, William Higgins Jr., Yakov Elizarov, Yvonne Gamble

VENEZUELA - Felix Bolivar

WESTERN SAHARA - Mohamed Beisat

YEMEN - Abdulaziz Bahaj

ZAMBIA - Mutoba Ngoma

Made in the USA
Columbia, SC
02 June 2021